ELECTRONIC WARFARE

Air Force Doctrine Document 3-13.1
5 November 2002

Incorporating Change 1, 28 July 2011

This document complements related discussion found in Joint Publication (JP) 1, *Doctrine for the Armed Forces of the United States*; and JP 3-0, *Joint Operations*.

Cover Sheet for Air Force Doctrine Document (AFDD) 3-13.1, *Electronic Warfare*

OPR: LeMay Center/DD

28 July 2011

AFDD numbering has changed to correspond with the joint doctrine publication numbering architecture (the AFDD titles remain unchanged until the doctrine is revised). Any AFDD citations within the documents will list the old AFDD numbers until the doctrine is revised. The changed numbers follow:

OLD	NEW	TITLE
AFDD 2-1	changed to AFDD 3-1	*Air Warfare*
AFDD 2-1.1	changed to AFDD 3-01	*Counterair Operations*
AFDD 2-1.2	changed to AFDD 3-70	*Strategic Attack*
AFDD 2-1.3	changed to AFDD 3-03	*Counterland Operations*
AFDD 2-1.4	changed to AFDD 3-04	*Countersea Operations*
AFDD 2-1.6	changed to AFDD 3-50	*Personnel Recovery Operations*
AFDD 2-1.7	changed to AFDD 3-52	*Airspace Control*
AFDD 2-1.8	changed to AFDD 3-40	*Counter-CBRN*
AFDD 2-1.9	changed to AFDD 3-60	*Targeting*
AFDD 2-10	changed to AFDD 3-27	*Homeland Operations*
AFDD 2-12	changed to AFDD 3-72	*Nuclear Operations*
AFDD 2-2	changed to AFDD 3-14	*Space Operations*
AFDD 2-2.1	changed to AFDD 3-14.1	*Counterspace Operations*
AFDD 2-3	changed to AFDD 3-24	*Irregular Warfare*
AFDD 2-3.1	changed to AFDD 3-22	*Foreign Internal Defense*
AFDD 2-4	changed to AFDD 4-0	*Combat Support*
AFDD 2-4.1	changed to AFDD 3-10	*Force Protection*
AFDD 2-4.2	changed to AFDD 4-02	*Health Services*
AFDD 2-4.4	changed to AFDD 4-11	*Bases, Infrastructure, and Facilities* [Rescinded]
AFDD 2-4.5	changed to AFDD 1-04	*Legal Support*
AFDD 2-5	changed to AFDD 3-13	*Information Operations*
AFDD 2-5.1	changed to AFDD 3-13.1	*Electronic Warfare*
AFDD 2-5.3	changed to AFDD 3-61	*Public Affairs Operations*
AFDD 2-6	changed to AFDD 3-17	*Air Mobility Operations*
AFDD 2-7	changed to AFDD 3-05	*Special Operations*
AFDD 2-8	changed to AFDD 6-0	*Command and Control*
AFDD 2-9	changed to AFDD 2-0	*ISR Operations*
AFDD 2-9.1	changed to AFDD 3-59	*Weather Operations*

SUMMARY OF CHANGES

This Interim change to Air Force Doctrine Document (AFDD) 2-5.1 changes the cover to AFDD 3-13.1, *Electronic Warfare* to reflect revised AFI 10-1301, Air Force Doctrine (9 August 2010). AFDD numbering has changed to correspond with the joint doctrine publication numbering architecture. AFDD titles and content remain unchanged until updated in the next full revision. A margin bar indicates newly revised material.

Supersedes: AFDD 2-5.1, 19 November 1999
OPR: LeMay Center/DD
Certified by: LeMay Center/DD (Col Todd C. Westhauser)
Pages: 58
Accessibility: Available on the e-publishing website at www.e-publishing.af.mil for
        downloading
Releasability: There are no releasability restrictions on this publication
Approved by: LeMay Center/CC, Maj Gen Thomas K. Anderson, USAF
        Commander, LeMay Center for Doctrine Development and Education

FOREWORD

Air and space power and technology have always been tightly bound together throughout the history of air and space operations. This linkage is very evident in the combat machines, devices, and tactics needed to survive in the air and space environment. The use of radio and radar early in World War II as the means to find targets on the surface and in the air illustrates the first technological exploitation of the electromagnetic (EM) spectrum in aerial warfare. The advent of countermeasures to these systems produced what we now consider electronic warfare (EW). Today's weapon systems and support systems rely on radio, radar, infrared (IR), electro-optical, ultraviolet, and laser technologies to function in peace and war. Unhampered use of the EM medium is vital to assure the success of any modern military operation. Coalition forces in Operation DESERT STORM operated "at will" over Iraq and Kuwait after gaining control of the EM spectrum early in the war. Air Force Doctrine Document (AFDD) 2-5.1, *Electronic Warfare*, provides a basis for understanding, planning, and executing this portion of air and space warfare.

DAVID F. MacGHEE, JR.
Major General, USAF
Commander, Air Force Doctrine Center

TABLE OF CONTENTS

INTRODUCTION

PURPOSE

This AFDD establishes operational doctrine for United States Air Force EW operations. It articulates fundamental Air Force principles for the application of combat force and provides commanders operational-level guidance on the employment and integration of Air Force resources to achieve desired objectives.

APPLICATION

This AFDD applies to all Air Force military and civilian personnel (includes AFRC and ANG units and members) involved in planning or conducting electronic warfare operations. The doctrine in this document is authoritative but not directive. Therefore, commanders need to consider not only the contents of this AFDD, but also the various issues relating to the particular situation in which they find themselves—national military objectives, forces available, enemy capabilities, rules of engagement (ROE)—when accomplishing their assigned missions.

SCOPE

This doctrine provides guidance for planning and conducting electronic warfare operations in support of national and joint force commander (JFC) campaign objectives.

FOUNDATIONAL DOCTRINE STATEMENTS

Foundational doctrine statements (FDS) are the basic principles and beliefs upon which AFDDs are built. Other information in the AFDDs expands on or supports these statements.

- Unfettered access to selected portions of the electromagnetic (EM) spectrum is critical for weapon system effectiveness and protection of critical air assets.

- EW is any military action involving the use of the EM spectrum to include directed energy (DE) to control the EM spectrum or to attack an enemy.

- EW is a force multiplier. EW operates on multiple levels of a conflict, from self-protection to operational attack plans. When EW actions are properly integrated with other military operations, a synergistic effect is achieved, losses minimized, and effectiveness enhanced.

- Control of the EM spectrum is an essential and critical objective in the success of today's military operations and is applicable at all levels of conflict.

- The decision to employ EW should be based not only on overall joint campaign or operation objectives, but also on the risks of possible adversary responses and other potential effects on the campaign or operation.

- Properly constructed force packages that includes EW enhances the probability of survival of all forces. It is unlikely that combat air and space operations will be able to completely avoid enemy defenses since they usually defend the desired targets.

- Senior officers must be well versed in the basic tenets of air and space EW employment and integration.

- EW impacts personnel in many areas to include: flight operations, air weapons, communications, intelligence, maintenance, security, and other operations and support functions.

- Operators must train against an integrated air defense system (IADS) that includes all types of threats: surface-to-air, air-to-air, and electronic warfare systems. "Train with EW. Fight with EW."

CHAPTER ONE

BACKGROUND

> *No enterprise is more likely to succeed than one concealed from the enemy until it is ripe for execution.*
>
> **Niccolo Machiavelli**
> *The Prince,* **1521**

Modern military forces rely heavily on a variety of complex, high technology, electronic offensive and defensive capabilities. EW is a specialized tool that enhances many air and space functions at multiple levels of conflict. Proper employment of EW enhances the ability of US operational commanders to achieve operational superiority over the adversary. Control of the electromagnetic (EM) spectrum has a major impact on the success of military operations. Modern weapons and support systems employ radio, radar, infrared (IR), optical, ultraviolet, electro-optical, and laser technologies. Commanders must prepare to operate weapons systems in an intensive and nonpermissive electromagnetic environment. This may be aggravated by both intentional and unintentional emissions from friendly, neutral, and enemy forces. Mission accomplishment requires awareness, dynamic planning, and flexibility at all levels of war. **Unfettered access to selected portions of the EM spectrum is critical for weapon system effectiveness and protection of critical air assets.**

Modern military systems, such as the E-8C joint surveillance, target attack radar system (JSTARS), rely on access to the electromagnetic spectrum to accomplish their missions.

EW is any military action involving the use of the EM spectrum to include directed energy (DE) to control the EM spectrum or to attack an enemy. This is not limited to radio or radar frequencies but includes IR, visible, ultraviolet, and other less used portions of the EM spectrum. EW assists air and space forces in gaining access to the battlespace and operating free

1

from interference from adversary threat systems. During Operation DESERT STORM, force packaging, which included self-protection, standoff, and escort jamming, and antiradiation attacks, significantly contributed to the Air Force's extremely low loss rate and astounding success rate against Iraqi forces.

Within the information operations (IO) construct, EW is an element of information warfare; more specifically, it is an element of offensive and defensive counterinformation (see figure 1.1). The three major components of EW are electronic attack (EA), electronic protection (EP), and electronic warfare support (ES). All three contribute to air and space operations, including the integrated IO effort. Control of the EM spectrum is gained by protecting friendly systems and attacking adversary systems. EA limits adversary use of the electronic spectrum; EP protects the use of the electronic spectrum for friendly forces; and ES enables the commander's accurate estimate of the situation in the operational area. All three must be carefully integrated to be effective. Therefore, commanders should ensure maximum integration among EW, intelligence, surveillance, and reconnaissance (ISR) and other IO functions.

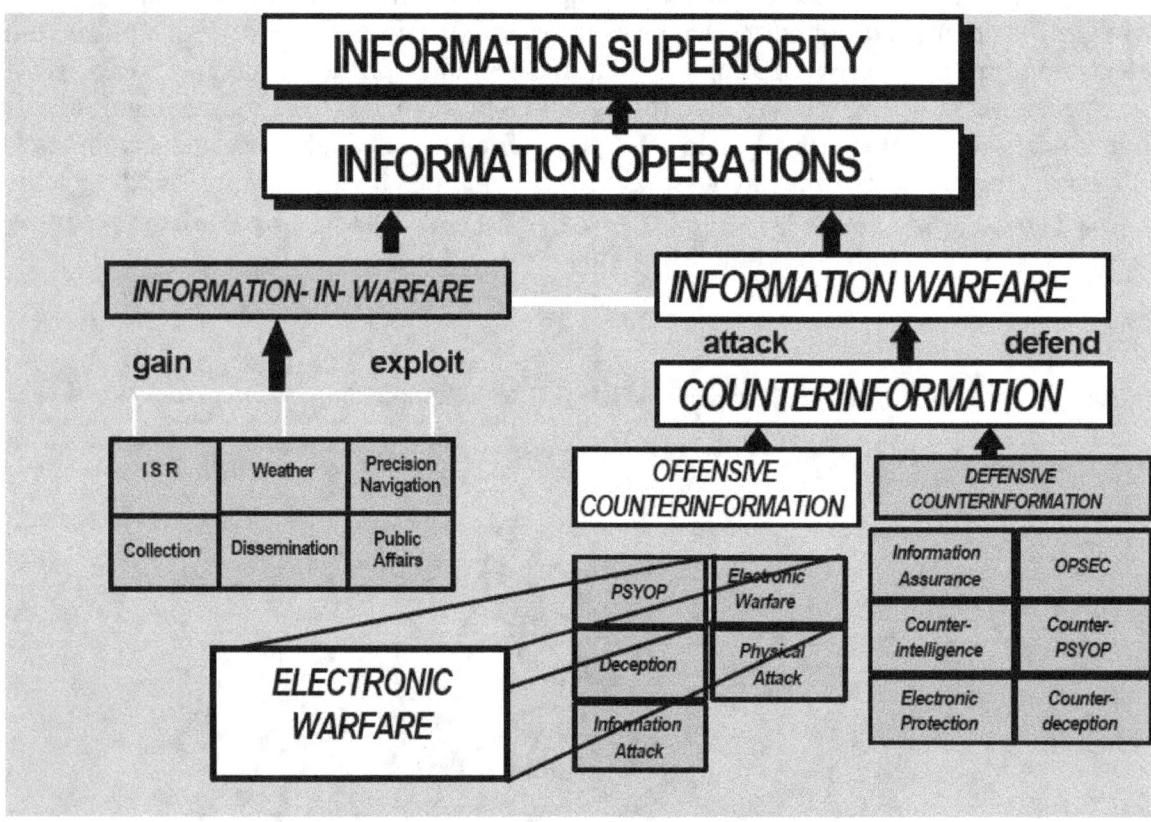

Figure 1.1. Information Operations Construct

Control of the EM spectrum can have a major impact on the success of military operations across the levels of conflict. Proper employment of EW enhances the ability of US operational commanders to achieve objectives. **EW is a force multiplier. EW operates on multiple levels of a conflict, from self-protection to operational attack plans. When EW actions are properly integrated with other military operations, a synergistic effect is achieved, losses minimized, and effectiveness enhanced.**

Air Force electronic warfare strategy embodies the art and science of employing military assets to improve operations through control of the EM spectrum. EW exploits weaknesses in an adversary's ability to operate and applies force against the adversary's offensive, defensive, and supporting capabilities across the EM spectrum. An effective EW strategy requires an integrated mix of passive, disruptive, and destructive systems to protect friendly weapon systems, components, and communications-electronics systems from the enemy's threat systems.

During the Gulf War, EF-111 RAVENS were used successfully against Iraqi radars and communications facilities.

Electronic warfare is intimately tied to advances in technology. The advent of radar and its proven effectiveness early in World War II started the "move–countermove" developments of radar, sensors, jammers, and countermeasures. Shortly after the development of radar, chaff was developed as a countermeasure. Concurrently, airborne jammers were developed to minimize the effectiveness of radar. The cold war witnessed the development of radar with effective electronic protection. Further EA developments were designed to defeat these protective measures. Conflicts in Vietnam and the Middle East provided deadly reminders of the necessity for effective EW against advanced threats and of the intense effort required to counter these threats. Current technology has given rise to new enemy capabilities, which includes the use of microwave and millimeter wave technologies, lasers, electro-optics, digital signal processing, and programmable and adaptable modes of operation. It also includes the use of IR, visible, and ultraviolet frequencies and that part of the electromagnetic spectrum where DE weapons might function. *Anticipating future technological developments is vital for EW and the survivability of friendly forces.*

EW in Vietnam

The EB-66 was used against terminal threat radars, surface-to-air missiles (SAMs), and antiaircraft artillery (AAA) until the development of self-defense pods on fighter aircraft. Then they were used as stand-off jamming platforms.

Countermeasures helped keep American aircraft losses to a manageable rate. One Air Force officer estimated that ECM [electronic countermeasures] reduced losses by 25 percent, while a Navy officer put the figure at 80 percent. Nevertheless, air operations were expensive both in losses and effort. Communist gunners proved a worthy and resourceful foe, although limited by second-rate Soviet equipment. Yet, despite the able Communist air defense tactics and their adaptation to the changing tactical situation, the American airmen gradually increased their edge. The big improvement for the offensive side came with the use of ECM and antiradiation and standoff weapons. These increased accuracy and decreased losses. In the full-scale operations of Linebacker II, the American airmen showed that massive application of modern aircraft with modern equipment could succeed against defenses limited in numbers and quality.

Kenneth P. Werrell
Archie, Flak, AAA, and SAM:
A Short Operational History of Ground-Based Air Defense

Control of the electromagnetic spectrum is an essential and critical objective in the success of today's military operations and is applicable at all levels of conflict. EW considerations must be coordinated into IO and fully integrated into operations in order to be effective. Friendly forces must prepare to operate in a nonpermissive EM environment and understand EW's potential to increase force effectiveness. Additionally, the scope of these operations is global and extends from the Earth's surface into space.

CHAPTER TWO

EW OPERATIONAL CONCEPTS

> *O divine art of subtlety and secrecy! Through you we learn to be invisible, through you inaudible; and hence hold the enemy's fate in our hands.*
>
> Sun Tzu,
> *The Art of War*, c. 500 B.C.

GENERAL

Military forces depend on the electromagnetic spectrum for many applications including, but not limited to, communications, detection, identification, and targeting. The effective application of electronic warfare in support of mission objectives is critical to the ability to find, fix, track, target, engage, and assess the adversary, while denying that adversary the same ability. Planners, operators, acquisition specialists, and others involved with Air Force EW must understand the technological advances and proliferation of threat systems in order to enable friendly use of the EM spectrum and protect the forces of the United States.

EW uses the tenets of control, exploit, and enhance to be effective. The three tenets are employed by the three components of EW: electronic attack (EA), electronic protection (EP), and electronic warfare support (ES). Proper application of these components produces the effects of detection, denial, disruption, deception, and destruction in varying degrees to enhance overall mission objectives.

Many countries around the world operate advanced surface-to-air missile systems, such as this SA-6.

EW TENETS

✪ **Control.** To control is to dominate the electromagnetic spectrum, directly or indirectly, so that friendly forces may attack the adversary and protect themselves from exploitation or attack.

✪ **Exploit.** To exploit is to use the electromagnetic spectrum to the advantage of friendly forces.

✪ **Enhance.** To enhance is to use EW as a force multiplier.

EW TENETS

Control

To control is to dominate the EM spectrum, directly or indirectly, so that friendly forces may exploit or attack the adversary and protect themselves from exploitation or attack. Electronic warfare has offensive and defensive aspects that work in a "move-countermove" fashion. Often, these aspects are used simultaneously and synergistically to support the mission. In the same way that air superiority allows friendly forces the freedom from attack, freedom to maneuver, and freedom to attack, the proper coordinated use of EW allows friendly forces to use the EM spectrum. As examples, the offensive denial of a command and control (C2) network by jamming disrupts the adversary's ability to marshal forces that would otherwise engage a friendly strike force. The proper use of EP allows friendly radar and communications to continue operating in the presence of enemy jamming.

Exploit

To exploit is to use the electromagnetic spectrum to the advantage of friendly forces. Friendly forces can use detection, denial, disruption, deception, and destruction in varying degrees to impede the adversary's decision loop. For instance, one may use electromagnetic deception to convey misleading information to an enemy or use an enemy's electromagnetic emissions to locate and identify the enemy. During the World War II, the United States tracked Japanese Navy ships by their radio transmissions. This usually provided the location, and since each radio operator had a unique touch, allowed Navy Intelligence to identify particular ships.

Enhance

To enhance is to use EW as a force multiplier. Careful integration of EW into air and space operations will detect, deny, disrupt, deceive, or destroy enemy forces in varying degrees to enhance overall mission effectiveness. Through proper control and exploitation of the EM spectrum, EW functions as a force multiplier and improves the likelihood of mission success. During the first night of Operation DELIBERATE FORCE, airborne jammers and antiradiation missiles negated adversary SAM systems, allowing North Atlantic Treaty Organization (NATO) aircraft unimpeded access to prime C2 targets in Bosnia.

ELECTRONIC WARFARE COMPONENTS

The three major components of EW are electronic attack (EA), electronic protection (EP), and electronic warfare support (ES). Figure 2.1 illustrates this concept, and the relationship between them.

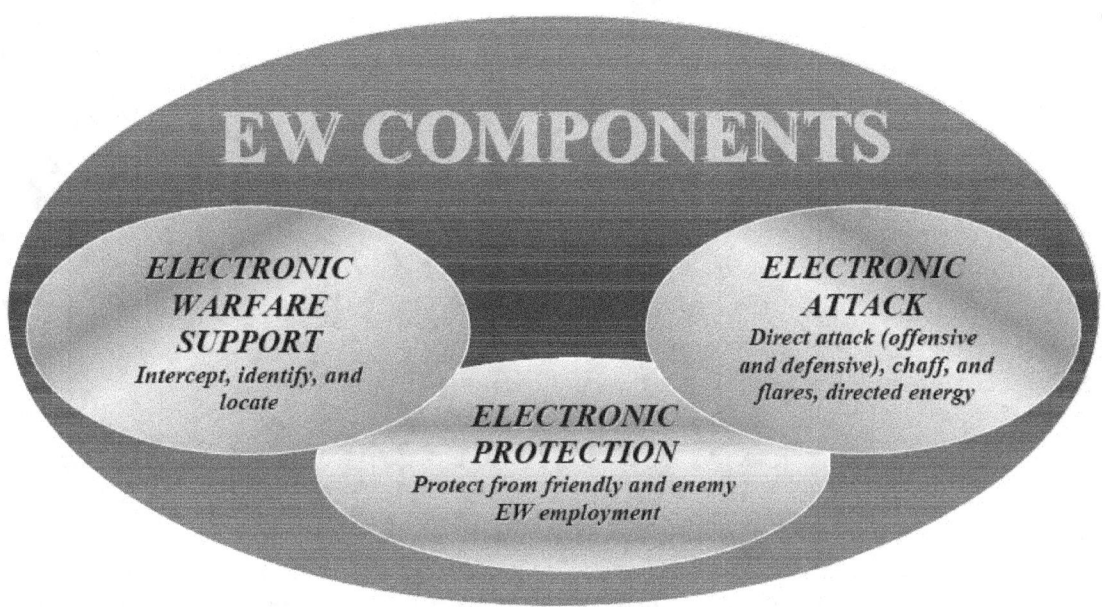

Figure 2.1 EW Components

Electronic Attack (EA)

EA Examples
✪ Standoff Jamming
✪ High-speed Antiradiation Missile (HARM)
✪ Chaff
✪ Flare
✪ Self-defense Jamming
✪ Directed Energy

EA is the component of EW involving the use of electromagnetic, directed energy, or antiradiation weapons to attack personnel, facilities, or equipment with the intent of degrading, neutralizing, or destroying enemy combat capability. EA also prevents or reduces an enemy's use of the electromagnetic spectrum. It can be accomplished through detection, denial, disruption, deception, and destruction. EA includes direct attack with high-speed antiradiation missiles (HARMs); active applications such as decoys, noise jamming, deceptive jamming, and expendable miniature jamming decoys; and employs EM or DE weapons (lasers, radio frequency weapons, particle beams, etc.). Electronic emission control (EMCON) and low observable technologies are passive applications of EA.

Electromagnetic jamming and the suppression of enemy air defenses (SEAD) are also applications of EA:

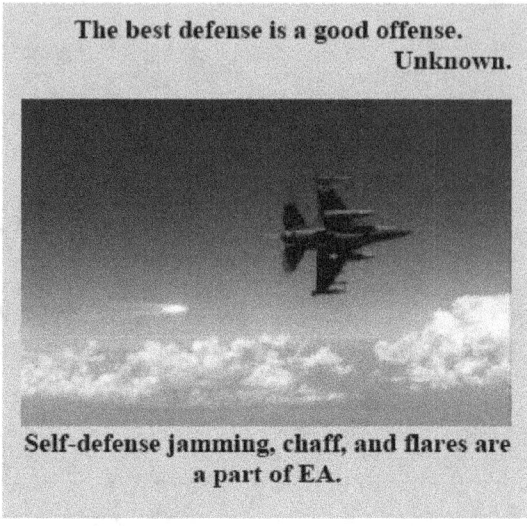

The best defense is a good offense.
Unknown.

Self-defense jamming, chaff, and flares are a part of EA.

✪ **EM Jamming. Electromagnetic jamming is the deliberate radiation, reradiation, or reflection of electromagnetic energy for the purpose of preventing or reducing an enemy's effective use of the electromagnetic spectrum, with the intent of degrading or neutralizing the enemy's combat capability.** Early Air Force EW efforts were primarily directed toward electronically jamming hostile radars to hide the number and location of friendly aircraft and to degrade the accuracy of radar-controlled weapons. Currently, jamming enemy sensor systems can limit enemy access to information on friendly force movements and composition and can cause confusion. Jamming can degrade the enemy's decision making and implementation process when applied against C2 systems. An adversary heavily dependent on centralized control and execution for force employment presents an opportunity for EA.

✪ **Suppression of Enemy Air Defenses (SEAD). SEAD is that activity which neutralizes, destroys, or temporarily degrades surface-based enemy air defenses by destructive and/or disruptive means.** The goal of SEAD operations is to provide a favorable situation in which friendly tactical forces can perform their missions effectively without interference from enemy air defenses. In Air Force doctrine, SEAD is not part of EW, but it is a broad term that may include the use of EW. In Air Force doctrine, SEAD is part of the counterair mission and directly contributes to obtaining air superiority. This may involve using electromagnetic radiation to neutralize, degrade, disrupt, delay, or

F-16CJ's use a high-speed antiradiation missile (HARM) targeting system and missiles to suppress or disable enemy radars.

destroy elements of an enemy's integrated air defense system (IADS). During hostilities, enemy air defensive systems will probably challenge friendly air operations. Weapon systems tasked to perform SEAD may be employed to locate and degrade, disrupt, neutralize, or destroy airborne and ground-based emitters. Normal SEAD targets include radars for early warning/ground-controlled intercept (EW/GCI), acquisition (ACQ), surface-to-air missiles (SAMs), and antiaircraft artillery (AAA). Many Air Force functions can be enhanced with the employment of SEAD operations.

Electronic Protection (EP)

EP EXAMPLES

⊗ **Frequency agility in a radio**

⊗ **Change pulse repetition frequency (PRF) on a radar set**

⊗ **Electronic and material shielding for systems**

⊗ **Processes to counter meaconing, interference, jamming, and intrusion (MIJI)**

EP includes the actions taken to protect personnel, facilities, and equipment from any EW employment that may degrade, neutralize, or destroy friendly combat capability. Examples of EP include frequency agility, changing pulse repetition frequency (PRF), etc. Integration of EP and other security measures can prevent enemy detection, denial, disruption, deception, or destruction. EP is part of defensive counterinformation (DCI) and needs to be properly integrated into the IO plan. Friendly force reliance on advanced technology demands comprehensive EP safeguards and considerations. Proper frequency management is a key element in preventing adverse effects (i.e., jamming friendly forces) by friendly forces. Much of the success of EP occurs during the design and acquisition of equipment.

Electronic Support (ES)

ES Examples

⊗ **Radar Warning Receivers**

⊗ **Communication Intelligence**

⊗ **Electronics Intelligence**

ES responds to taskings to search for, intercept, identify, and locate sources of intentional and unintentional radiated electromagnetic energy for the purpose of threat recognition. Commanders, aircrews, and operators use ES to provide near-real-time information to supplement information from other intelligence sources. Additionally, ES information can be correlated with other ISR information to provide a more accurate picture of the battlespace. This information can be developed into an electronic order of battle (EOB) for situational awareness and may be used to develop new countermeasures. The relationship between ES and signals intelligence (SIGINT), which includes electronic

The RC-135 provides surveillance and reconnaissance information

intelligence (ELINT) and communications intelligence (COMINT), is closely related because they share the common functions of search, interception, identification, location, and exploitation of electromagnetic radiation. The distinction lies in the type and use of information and who has tasking authority. ES resources are tasked by or under direct control of operational commanders. The operational commander may have authority to task national SIGINT assets to provide ES or may have direct operational control over tactical resources capable of providing ES. In either case, ES is distinguished by the fact that the operational commander determines aspects of resource configuration required to provide ES that meets immediate operational requirements. SIGINT is tasked by national authorities. The passive nature of ES allows it to be effectively employed during peacetime.

EW EFFECTS

EW Effects

✪ **Detection**—Assesses the electromagnetic environment to include radar/radio frequency, electro-optics/laser, and infared spectrums using active and passive means.

✪ **Denial**—Controls the information an adversary receives and prevents the adversary from gaining accurate information about friendly forces.

✪ **Deception**—Utilizes the electromagnetic spectrum to confuse or mislead an adversary.

✪ **Disruption**—Degrades or interferes with the enemy's control of it's forces in order to limit attacks on friendly forces.

✪ **Destruction**—Eliminates some or all of an adversary's electronic defenses.

EW is waged throughout the electromagnetic spectrum to secure and maintain effective control and use through the integration of detection, denial, deception, disruption, and destruction. The operational application of EW is not limited to manned airborne application; it is also applied from land and space by manned and unmanned vehicles. While control of the EM spectrum through the proper application of EW is advantageous, when improperly used without coordination it may heighten the risk to friendly forces. An ill-timed jamming package may highlight an otherwise unseen force or deny the use of a frequency by friendly forces. An incorrect or wrongly interpreted radar warning receiver (RWR) indication may cause an inappropriate action to be taken. The proper employment of EW involves various applications of detection, denial, deception, disruption, and destruction.

The EA-6B is a joint EW platform that can detect threats, provide standoff jamming, and can carry HARMs.

Detection

Detection is assessing the electromagnetic environment to include radar/radio frequency, electro-optics/laser, and the IR spectrums using active and passive means. It is the first step in EW because effective mapping of the electromagnetic environment is essential to develop an accurate electronic order of battle (EOB). The EOB is critical for EW decision making and for using the electromagnetic spectrum to meet mission objectives. The various means of detection include on-board receivers, space-based systems, unmanned aerial vehicles (UAV), human intelligence (HUMINT), and other ISR systems. Detection supports EA, EP, and ES, and enables the avoidance of known hostile systems. When avoidance is not possible, it may become necessary to deny, deceive, disrupt, or destroy the enemy's electronic systems.

Denial

Denial is controlling the information an enemy or adversary receives, preventing the acquisition of accurate information about friendly forces. For example, denial can be done by traditional noise jamming techniques designed to block communications channels or radarscope presentations. Denial may also be accomplished through more advanced electronic deception techniques or destructive measures. The EC-130H COMPASS CALL provides an excellent denial example as the Air Force's premier communications jamming weapon. A discriminate electronic attack asset, it has the ability to deny enemy communication while allowing friendly communications to remain unhindered.

Deception

Deception is confusing or misleading an adversary. One objective of EW is to exploit the decision-making loop of the opposition through use of the electromagnetic spectrum, making it difficult to distinguish between reality and the perception of reality. If an adversary relies on electromagnetic sensors to gather intelligence, deceptive information can be channeled into these systems to mislead and confuse. Deception efforts must stimulate as many adversary information sources as possible to achieve the desired objective. Multisensor deception can increase the adversary's confidence about the "plausibility" of the deception story. Deception efforts are coordinated with the military deception officer and considered during development of an overall deception plan, IO plan, and the overall campaign plan. Operational security is critical to an effective deception plan.

Electromagnetic deception as it applies to EW is the deliberate radiation, reradiation, alteration, suppression, absorption, denial, enhancement, or reflection of EM energy in a manner intended to convey misleading information to an enemy or to enemy EM-dependent weapons, thereby degrading or neutralizing the enemy's combat capability. Deception jammers/transmitters can place false targets on the enemy radar's scope, or cause the enemy radar to assess incorrect target speed, range, or azimuth. Such jammers/transmitters operate by receiving the pulse of energy from the radar, amplifying it, delaying or multiplying it, and reradiating the altered signal back to the enemy's transmitting radar.

Types of Electromagnetic Deception

✪ Manipulative Electromagnetic Deception

✪ Simulative Electromagnetic Deception

✪ Imitative Electromagnetic Deception

Manipulative EM deception involves an action to eliminate revealing or to convey misleading EM telltale indicators that may be used by hostile forces. An example of this is to mislead the enemy by transmitting a simulated unique system signature from a nonlethal platform, thereby allowing the enemy sensors to receive and catalog those systems as actual threats in the area. Low observable technology is a passive form of manipulative electromagnetic deception. By passively manipulating or denying the threat radar from receiving proper return pulses, it alters the perceived size or presence of an aerospace vehicle. EM deception can use communication or noncommunication signals to convey indicators that mislead the enemy. It can also cause the enemy to splinter their intelligence and EW efforts to the point that they will lose their effectiveness. Manipulative electromagnetic deception can be used to cause the enemy to misdirect ES and EA assets and, therefore, cause fewer problems with friendly communications. In this application it is an EP technique.

Simulative electromagnetic deception is action to simulate friendly, notional, or actual capabilities to mislead hostile forces. Examples of simulative electromagnetic detection are: the use of chaff to simulate false targets so that the enemy has the impression of a larger strike package or the use of a jammer to transmit a deceptive technique that misleads an adversary's target tracking radar so that it cannot find the true location of its target.

ECM and the Normandy Landing

'Window' was also employed during the D-day landings. On D-day minus 2, the coast of Northern France presented a solid radar front—an active threat to invasion operations. Between Ostend and Cherbourg, there was a major German radar station every 10 miles. Actual count from Brest to Calais showed 6 Chimneys and 6 Hoardings for long-range early warning, 38 Freyas for medium range EW and night fighter control, 42 Giant Wurzburgs for night fighter control and coast gun control for use against low flying aircraft, 17 Coastwatchers, and Small Wurzburgs, one per flak battery.

The first task on D-day was to confuse what remained of the German early warning radar (EWR) system which still posed a formidable threat to operations of Allied troop carrier and tug [aircraft towing gliders] aircraft.

On the night preceding D-day, the confusion was accomplished by Mandrel (anti-Freya) jammers carried in eight Sterling aircraft along the south coast, and in four B-17s spaced to give cover as far as the island of Guernsey. Flying at 18,000 feet for 5 hours, these squadrons screened the approach of airborne forces to the French coast.

Meanwhile, British Bomber Command aircraft carried jammers and dropped Window [chaff] and dummy parachutists inland from the Dover-Calais area. Reacting to these countermeasures, German fighter strength spent most of the night circling over the Calais area. As a result, there were no fighter attacks on the 884 transports and 105 gliders of the 9th Troop Carrier Command, which landed or dropped some 15,000 troops.

Electronic Combat Principles
AFP 51-45
15 September 1987

Imitative EM deception introduces EM energy into enemy systems that imitate enemy emissions. Any enemy receiver can be the target of imitative electromagnetic deception. This might be used to screen friendly operations. An example is the use of a repeater jamming technique that imitates enemy radar pulses. These pulses, when received by the tracking radar, input incorrect target information into the enemy's system.

Self-defense jamming pods, such as the ALQ-184, use various deception techniques.

Other examples of deception include IR deception involving manipulation of infrared signatures; radar deception consisting of reradiation of signals through the use of reflectors, transponders, or repeaters; and optical deception by manipulation of the optical region of the EM spectrum through the use of aerosols, mists, etc. These techniques may be employed individually or in combination. In general, EW deception planning determines how to use EM means to mislead the adversary and create an advantage for friendly forces.

Disruption

Disruption is degrading or interfering with the enemy's use of the EM spectrum to limit the enemy's combat capabilities. Disruption is achieved by using electronic jamming, electronic deception, electronic intrusion, and destruction. These will enhance attacks against hostile forces and act as a force multiplier.

Destruction

When used in the EW context, destruction is the elimination of some or all of an adversary's electronic defenses. It is the most permanent countermeasure. Target tracking radars and C2 are high value targets because their destruction seriously hampers the enemy's effectiveness. Destruction requires determining the exact location of the target. This location may be found through the effective application of ES measures. Onboard receivers and direction finding equipment may pinpoint the location of the target. Enemy EM systems can be destroyed by a variety of weapons and techniques, ranging from bombardment with conventional munitions to intense radiation and high energy particle beam overloading. Destruction of enemy EM equipment may be the most effective means of denying the enemy the use of the EM spectrum. The length of suppression will depend on the enemy's capability to repair and replace combat assets. An example of EW application of destruction would be the use of a high-speed antiradiation missile (HARM) against an enemy radar.

ADDITIONAL FACTORS

Directed Energy (DE) in EW

DE is an umbrella term covering technologies that relate to the production of a beam of concentrated electromagnetic energy or atomic or subatomic particles. Directed-energy warfare (DEW) is military action involving the use of DE weapons, devices, and countermeasures to either cause direct damage or destruction of enemy equipment, facilities, and personnel, or to determine, exploit, reduce, or prevent hostile use of the EM spectrum through damage, destruction, and disruption. It also includes actions taken to protect friendly equipment, facilities, and personnel and to retain friendly use of the EM spectrum (JP 1-02). Applications of DE include: laser, radio frequency, and particle beam. DE can be applied to conduct EA, ES, or EP. For example, a laser designed to blind or disrupt optical sensors is EA. A warning receiver designed to detect and analyze a laser signal is ES. A visor or goggle designed to filter out the harmful wavelength of laser light is EP.

1973 Arab-Israeli War

The 1973 Arab-Israeli War lasted less than a month, yet it contained all the elements of a much longer war.

The 1973 Arab-Israeli War lasted less than a month, yet it contained all the elements of a much longer war. It was an intense, bitterly contested conflict with each side well equipped with the weapons for modern warfare. The Egyptian and Syrian air defenses at that time were developed from Soviet design. The design stressed overlapping networks of SAM and AAA coverage. This formidable air defense network consisted of the SA-2, SA-3, SA-6, SA-7, the ZSU-23-4, and other AAA systems. While there were proven ECM from the Vietnam War for the SA-2 and SA-3 and infrared (IR) countermeasures, such as flares for the SA-7, the SA-6 proved to be a surprise. The SA-6's radars operated in a portion of the EM spectrum never used before by the Soviets. The Israelis tried to compensate for their lack of ECM against the SA-6 by flying lower, trying to get under its radar coverage. This tactic placed them into the heart of the ZSU-23-4 threat envelope and contributed to the loss of numerous aircraft. This forced the Israelis to adjust their electronic equipment, modify their tactics, and seek additional ECM equipment, such as ECM pods and chaff dispensers from the US.

However, before the tactics were changed and the new equipment arrived, the Israelis suffered heavy aircraft losses, which taught them a valuable lesson. They learned ECM [EA] is an essential and vital part of the SEAD campaign.

Electronic Combat Principles
AFP 51-45
15 September 1987

Enemy Capabilities

Commanders must know their own EW capabilities and those of potential enemies. Mission planning hinges on accurate information. Each year, new technology weapons systems are fielded in increasing numbers. Potential adversaries recognize US dependence on electronically oriented communications and weapons systems. Seeking to take advantage of this fact, some potential adversaries are organized to attack our critical weapons systems control functions and associated communications nodes. Many countries have been purchasing modern and capable weapons systems from a variety of sources. In addition, terrorists may acquire highly sophisticated and dangerous weapons. To counter these possibilities, commanders and their staff must become well versed in the employment of weapons systems and the EW capabilities of all possible adversaries.

Operational Requirements

The level of EW involvement will always depend on the specific requirements of the mission. Electronic warfare is task oriented. Operational objectives, the tactical situation, the effectiveness and availability of combat systems, and the prevailing domestic and international political climate determine the appropriate application of military resources. EW planning is not just the automatic addition of a specific jamming pod or escort package for a mission. Each task may require a specific EW response in order to achieve a desired objective. Commanders and their staffs must consider the threat and assets available to support EW objectives.

Intelligence, Surveillance, and Reconnaissance (ISR)

The key to successful military operations is a thorough knowledge of enemy capabilities derived from near-real-time information, focused for the operational commander, as well as long term operational, scientific, and technical intelligence information gathered over a period of time. Knowledge of the enemy's projected military capabilities is required to avoid surprise. Accurate intelligence is needed to gauge the intent of an adversary, and this intelligence must be transmitted to the users in a timely manner. Numerous surveillance and reconnaissance systems are used to collect the data needed to build the various electronic databases required to effectively employ EW. Advanced processing and exploitation systems, with man-in-the-loop management and oversight, transform the data into usable intelligence, while survivable communications grids bring the intelligence to the operational user. As in all military operations, defining and managing intelligence requirements are critical to EW

Environmental Conditions

The natural environment also affects the use of the EM spectrum. These effects occur over the entire spectrum. Clouds, sun glint, ground reflections, moisture, and dust can degrade performance of systems operating in the IR and optical frequencies. Atmospheric conditions can distort radar signals causing track errors, extending the detection ranges or creating "holes" in radar coverage. Rain and frozen precipitation also affects microwave transmissions by

UAVs like PREDATOR may be used for EA and/or ES in the future.

attenuating and scattering the signal. Even disturbances on the sun and in the upper atmosphere can create radio frequency interference (RFI) in radars and satellite links, impact high-frequency radio and satellite communications, and degrade ground positioning system (GPS) accuracy. Planners using forecasts of terrestrial and space environmental conditions can exploit or mitigate these effects to their advantage over an adversary.

CONCLUSION

Electronic warfare through effective use of detection, denial, deception, disruption, and destruction provides timely intelligence, enhances combat power by disrupting the enemy's use of the electromagnetic spectrum at critical times, and ensures continued friendly use of the electromagnetic spectrum. The synergistic effects of various EW techniques can significantly disrupt an IADS, sensors, communication links, weapon systems, and C2. Jamming, chaff, and decoys degrade the enemy's ability to find, fix, track, target, engage, and assess. Radar-guided weapon systems that survive destruction attempts lose some effectiveness in an EW environment. In short, the probability of success is greatly increased when EW is properly employed. Electronic warfare is a key element in the successful employment of air and space forces.

CHAPTER THREE

ELECTRONIC WARFARE ORGANIZATION

Never tell people how to do things. Tell them what to do and they will surprise you with their ingenuity.

General George S. Patton

GENERAL

EW assets are organized on the air and space tenet of centralized control and decentralized execution. Air Force EW resources are normally employed as part of an air and space expeditionary task force (AETF) and exercised at the lowest level providing responsiveness to the Commander, Air Force Forces (COMAFFOR). Appropriate EW expertise must be available at all levels of command where EW coordination, planning, and tasking occur.

JOINT AND MULTINATIONAL OPERATIONS

Joint and multinational plans must be developed for integrating EW activities. Close coordination between coalition partners, Services, air traffic control facilities, civil defense activities, and war-related commerce departments is essential for EW application to be effective and not interfere with friendly forces. This is required to ensure maximum support, prevent mutual interference, define mutually supporting roles, avoid duplication of effort, and provide security. The importance of integration and coordination cannot be overemphasized, particularly since technological advances are increasing the complexity and interdependence of combat operations. The required deconfliction and coordination of airborne and space-based EW support should be accomplished at the joint air operations center (JAOC), or at the combined air operations center (CAOC), which works in coordination with the joint task force (JTF). Considerations must include the impact of EW on C2, other information operations, and interrelated requirements for use of the EM spectrum. Specific guidance on organization and procedures is covered in JP 3-51, *Joint Doctrine for Electronic Warfare.*

The number of specialized EW assets is usually limited; therefore, operational control of these forces should not be delegated lower than the joint force air component commander (JFACC). The JAOC is notionally organized as illustrated in figure 3.1. Wing and unit level staffs and individual aircrews develop the detailed tactical planning for specific EW missions. Individual operators must keep current in systems employment and the threat.

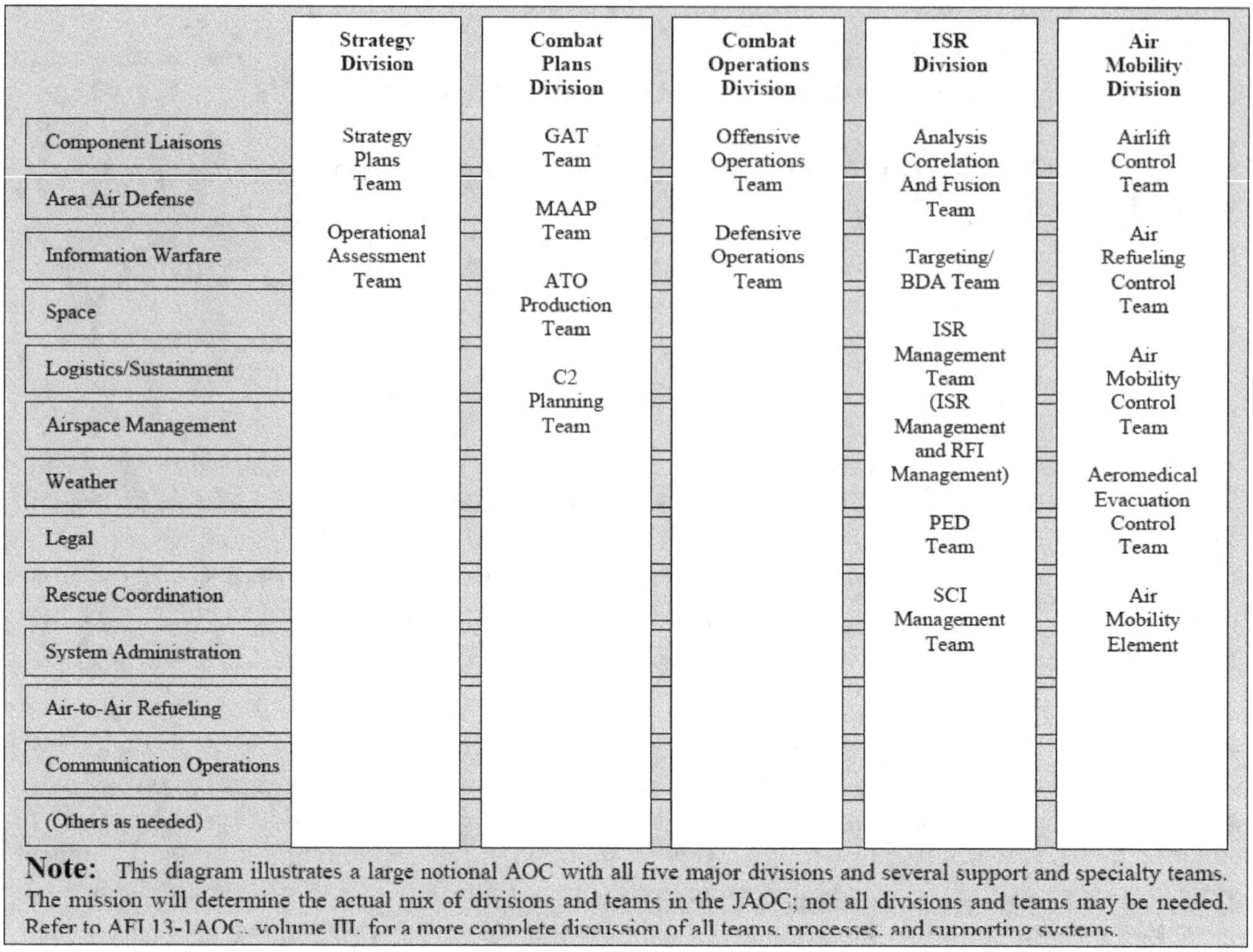

	Strategy Division	Combat Plans Division	Combat Operations Division	ISR Division	Air Mobility Division
Component Liaisons	Strategy Plans Team	GAT Team	Offensive Operations Team	Analysis Correlation And Fusion Team	Airlift Control Team
Area Air Defense		MAAP Team	Defensive Operations Team	Targeting/ BDA Team	Air Refueling Control Team
Information Warfare	Operational Assessment Team	ATO Production Team		ISR Management Team (ISR Management and RFI Management)	Air Mobility Control Team
Space					
Logistics/Sustainment		C2 Planning Team			
Airspace Management					
Weather					Aeromedical Evacuation Control Team
Legal				PED Team	
Rescue Coordination				SCI Management Team	Air Mobility Element
System Administration					
Air-to-Air Refueling					
Communication Operations					
(Others as needed)					

Note: This diagram illustrates a large notional AOC with all five major divisions and several support and specialty teams. The mission will determine the actual mix of divisions and teams in the JAOC; not all divisions and teams may be needed. Refer to AFI 13-1AOC, volume III, for a more complete discussion of all teams, processes, and supporting systems.

Figure 3.1. Notional JAOC with Representative Core, Specialty, and Support Teams

JAOC/CAOC PLANNING AND EXECUTION PROCESS

Fundamental to the JAOC is an integrated team controlled by the JAOC director. Within the JAOC, the EW staff officer or the EW branch of the Combat Plans Division (CPD) (depending on JAOC manning and organization) normally has primary responsibility for air and space EW planning and integration into the air and space assessment, planning, and execution

process (see figure 3.2) that produces the air tasking order (ATO) for the JTF and monitors its execution. Individual wing commanders will provide an EW point of contact who may be the wing electronic warfare officer (EWO), wing defensive systems officer (DSO), or wing electronic combat officer (ECO) as the EW representative to the JAOC for the respective wing's weapon platform(s). The wing EW representatives plan for available EW equipment employment and oversee radar warning receiver and other EW systems reprogramming.

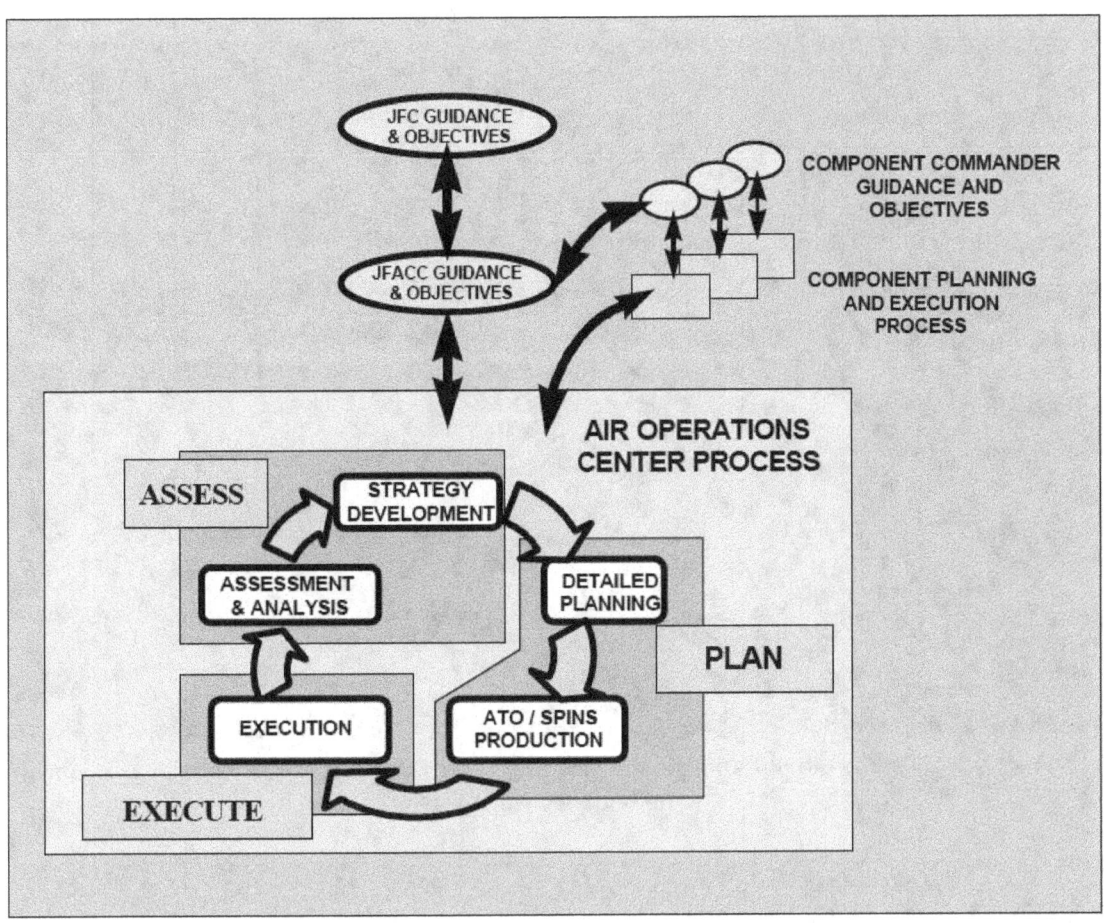

Figure 3.2. The Air and Space Assessment, Planning, and Execution Process

The JAOC EW staff officer or other personnel supporting the EW (CPD) branch typically integrates with the IO cell that coordinates all IO actions within the JAOC. The EW representative of the IO cell could be the same as the EW representative of the CPD, but more likely would be a separate EW staff representative trained to facilitate the coordination of EW with other disciplines of IO. Essentially, the JAOC EW staff officer or the CPD EW branch oversees Air Force Service component asset issues while the IO EW representative coordinates broader IO across the Services as a representative of the designated A-3/J-3. The IO cell is charged with coordinating the offensive and defensive aspects of IO to include special programs and integrating IO efforts with the joint air operations plan (JAOP). Those individuals should represent all aspects of air and space EW planning and execution and work closely with the intelligence personnel. The interface between the JAOC EW representative and the IO cell ensures that all aspects of EW are fully integrated into strategy development, operational-level assessment, detailed planning, ATO production, and execution functions.

The JAOC is at the heart of coordinating air and space planning, execution, and assessment, to include electronic warfare.

EW SUPPORT TO THE JOINT FORCE AIR AND SPACE COMPONENT COMMANDER (JFACC)

The joint force commander (JFC) will normally designate a JFACC to exploit the capabilities of joint air and space operations through a cohesive JAOP and a responsive and integrated control system. The JFC must clearly define EW objectives and ensure that assets supporting these objectives are properly employed and integrated throughout military operations. The JAOC formulates plans and coordinates air and space EW activities based on the JFACC's guidance, which is based on JFC objectives. It receives, assembles, analyzes, processes, and disseminates all source intelligence required for air and space EW planning. Airborne and space-based EW support assets are normally tasked through the ATO. EW planners will support the JFACC as follows:

✪ Develop a joint EW strategy.

✪ Task, plan, coordinate, and allocate the joint EW capabilities/forces made available to the JFACC by direction of the JFC and provide EW support to the Air Force functions.

✪ Perform combat assessment of joint EW operations at the operational and tactical levels.

✪ Provide integrated ES for the JFC.

　　✪ ✪ Identify JFACC requirements.

✪ ✪ Integrate and synchronize use of air and space assets.

✪ ✪ Task theater ES assets to satisfy JFC requirements.

If working with allies in a coalition, the EW team will support the Combined Force Air Component Commander (CFACC).

EW SUPPORT TO THE COMMANDER, AIR FORCE FORCES (COMAFFOR)

The COMAFFOR provides unity of command, one of the most widely recognized principles of war. The COMAFFOR normally exercises operational control (OPCON) over all assigned and attached US Air Force forces. EW planners will assist the COMAFFOR in fulfilling the following administrative control (ADCON) responsibilities:

✪ Make recommendations to the JFC (or the JFACC, if the COMAFFOR is not the JFACC) on the proper employment of the EW forces of the Air Force component.

✪ Accomplish assigned EW tasks.

✪ Nominate specific EW units of the Air Force for assignment to theater forces.

✪ Maintain reach back to Air Force forces (AFFOR) rear and to the supporting Air Force EW units.

✪ Support operations and exercise EW plans as requested.

✪ Inform the combatant commander (and any intermediate JFCs) of EW program and budget decisions that may affect joint operation planning.

✪ Provide lateral EW interface with Army, Navy, Marines, special operations forces (SOF), and coalition partners.

When the COMAFFOR is delegated OPCON of the Air Force component forces, and there is no JFACC, EW planners will assist the COMAFFOR in fulfilling the following OPCON responsibilities:

✪ Prepare an EW estimate of the situation to support the JFC's estimate.

✪ Develop and recommend EW courses of action to the JFC.

✪ Develop an EW strategy and an operations plan that state how the COMAFFOR plans to exploit EW capabilities to support the JFC's objectives.

✪ Make EW apportionment recommendations to the JFC.

✪ Task, plan, coordinate, and allocate the daily airborne and space-based EW effort.

✪ Function as the integrator for EW for counterair operations, strategic attack, the overall air interdiction effort, space support, and theater airborne reconnaissance and surveillance.

✪ Function as the EW interface, as directed by the JFC, for operations such as close air support, air interdiction within the land and naval component area of operations (AOs), and maritime support.

✪ Coordinate EW support for combat search and rescue.

✪ Provide electronic database and communications network support.

✪ Conduct joint EW training of components of other Services as directed, in joint operations for which the COMAFFOR has or may be assigned primary responsibility, or for which the Air Force component's facilities and capabilities are suitable.

COMAFFOR HEADQUARTERS ORGANIZATION: THE "A" STAFF

The COMAFFOR headquarters is usually comprised of normal staff directorates (see figure 3.3), A-1 through A-6, as well as a special staff. In deliberate planning or crisis action planning, the numbered air force (NAF) who is normally designated as the COMAFFOR will integrate EW experts into the organization. More details are available in AFDD 2, *Organization and Employment of Aerospace Power.* The core of the EW function is located in the A-3 as part of the JAOC and its IO cell. The entire IO operation must be integrated with A-2/3/5/6. The EW personnel will provide these functions:

Intelligence (A-2)

✪ Provide to the intelligence staff the A-2 related EW objectives, intent, and plans.

✪ Coordinate EW intelligence support from JFC fusion centers, major command (MAJCOM) intelligence staffs, theater intelligence agencies, national intelligence agencies, and coalition intelligence sources.

Operations/Plans (A-3/A-5)

✪ Organize the operational EW aspects of the headquarters staff.

✪ Coordinate operational EW issues with the JFC and component staffs. Typical issues would include:

    ✪ ✪ Rules of engagement for EW air and space forces.

- ✪ ✪ Assist in unit bed down requirements for air and space EW forces.

- ✪ ✪ EW development requirements for ATO and airspace control order (ACO).

- ✪ ✪ Requirements for additional EW forces/capabilities.

- ✪ ✪ Requirements for force protection.

- ✪ Identify essential elements of information (EEI) to A-2.

- ✪ Apprise the ISR team chief of EW capabilities and limitations of all components and the potential effects on operations.

- ✪ Assist ISR team chief with EW intelligence support requirements of subordinate units.

- ✪ Develop and coordinate the EW plan and integrate it into the IO plan that accomplishes the JFC's objectives.

- ✪ Identify Service-specific EW training requirements and coordinate joint training with other components.

- ✪ Advise COMAFFOR on concepts of EW employment, force planning, and management of EW resources for which he has OPCON/tactical control (TACON) or has established supported/supporting relationships.

- ✪ Provide information on the number and location of all EW air and space assets.

Communications and Information (A-6)

- ✪ Coordinate for the A-3 to ensure that frequency allocations and assignments meet technical parameters under host-nation agreements.

- ✪ Deconflict frequencies and coordinate the joint restricted frequency list (JRFL) with J-6.

- ✪ Provide communications-electronics operating instructions for assigned air and space forces.

- ✪ Plan, coordinate, and monitor EW related communications security (COMSEC) procedures and assets.

CHAPTER FOUR

PLANNING AND EMPLOYMENT

> *To achieve victory we must as far as possible make the enemy blind by sealing his eyes and ears, and drive his commanders to distraction by creating confusion in their minds.*
>
> Mae Tse Tung

PLANNING

General

EW planning requires a broad understanding of enemy and friendly capabilities, tactics, and objectives (see figure 4.1). Employment of EW assets must be closely integrated into, and supportive of, the commander's overall planning effort. This planning requires a multidisciplined approach with expertise from operations (ground, airborne, space), intelligence, logistics, weather, and information.

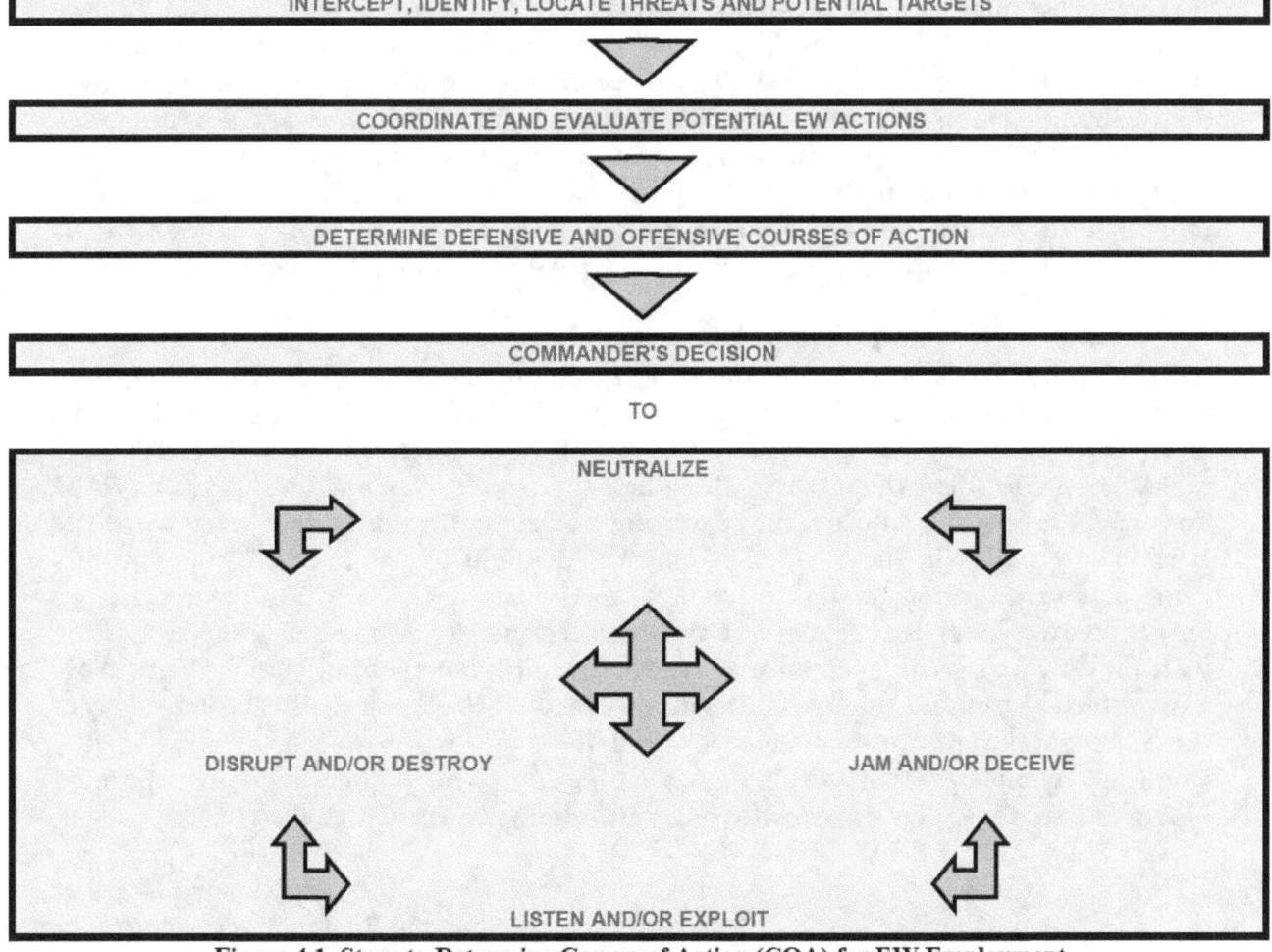

Figure 4.1. Steps to Determine Course of Action (COA) for EW Employment

MH-53J PAVE LOW

Early in the morning of 17 January 1991, three US Air Force MH-53J PAVE LOW helicopters led nine US Army AH-64 Apache helicopters across the Saudi Arabia-Iraq border to attack two Iraqi early warning radar sites. Taking down these two sites opened the door for attacks across Iraq by F-117s, other coalition aircraft and Tomahawk missiles.

After the F-117s and cruise missiles came conventional aircraft. From 0355L to 0420L (H+55 to H+1:20) large numbers of USAF, USN, USMC, RSAF, and RAF aircraft smashed Iraqi air defenses and fields from H-3, an airfield located in western Iraq, to Ahmed Al Jaber, an airfield in occupied Kuwait. Two packages of aircraft, one a USN package from the Red Sea carriers and the other a USAF package from the south pointed directly at Baghdad. These "gorilla" packages were intended to seem threatening enough to force the Iraqis to hurl their air resources in defense. Air Force ground-launched BQM-34 and Navy tactical air-launched decoys (TALD) mimicked the radar return of conventional aircraft to further arouse Iraqi radar operators, many already confused by the absence of central control from Kari. They responded by turning on their equipment. Finally, radar-jamming aircraft radiated blanketing electronic emissions that drove the Iraqi radar operators to go to full power in an attempt to break through the interference. Then, the two incoming coalition flights revealed their true nature and pounced in a shrewd and devastating ruse.

Instead of bomb-carrying fighter-bombers, they were radar-killing electronic warriors carrying AGM-88 high-speed antiradiation missiles (HARMS) designed to home in on SAM and AAA radar. USAF F-4G Wild Weasels alone expended dozens of HARMS in twenty minutes, while USN/USMC F/A-18s fired one hundred for the night. HARMS filled the air over Baghdad, the site of over one-half of Iraq's SAM and AAA batteries. Foolishly, the Iraqis did not turn off their radars, even when the HARMS fireballed in their midst; as one USAF flight leader averred, 'the emitters came on and stayed on for the entire flight of the missiles.' This deadly surprise not only destroyed many Iraqi radars, it also terrified their operators. For the rest of the war, they showed great reluctance to use radar and often chose to launch their SAMs with optical or even no guidance. The initial HARM attack and the F-117 bombings of the Kari system left Iraq's integrated air defense system shattered, opening up the country so completely that, within days, coalition air-to-air tankers regularly operated in Iraqi airspace. Other non-stealthy aircraft pummeled Iraqi airfields.

Richard G. Davis

Decisive Force: Strategic Bombing in the Gulf War

Planning Requirements

As a conflict progresses, adjustments will be necessary based on current intelligence. Proper EW planning can minimize friendly losses and optimize operational effectiveness. Preconflict plans should cover all long-range possibilities. Accordingly, preparation is not under pressure caused by enemy initiatives. An assessment of enemy and friendly capabilities is fundamental for preconflict planning. These plans should integrate the C2 strategy, air defense targeting, and plans to support primary mission resources. EW support to primary mission aircraft will depend on where friendly aircraft are at critical times. This support should consider detection, deception, denial, disruptive, and destructive systems capabilities. The C2 and air defense prioritized target list must be integrated into the overall prioritized target list. How and when these targets are attacked depends on the apportionment and allocation process, as determined by the JFC's objective. The EW plan should be optimized against enemy system vulnerabilities. Factors influencing EW planning include available assets; desired effects (exploitation, deception, disruption, or destruction); placement limitations (altitude, range, time, or loads); frequency deconfliction; anticipated EW missions from other Services; and authentication requirements.

Planning Priorities

As with any operation, the JFC's objective, enemy situation, and available assets will impact on the priority for employment of EW assets. EW is task, scenario, and time dependent. The commander's EW plans must be flexible to keep pace with the dynamic combat environment.

Force Mix Considerations

A balance is necessary between dedicated and self-protection EW systems as well as between the different EW effects. The commander's objectives, the enemy's capabilities, and the equipment available determine the actual force mix. Considerations include the threat, tactics, attrition rates, regeneration factors, friendly and enemy sortie rates, technological risks, and warning times. The effectiveness of offensive electronic assets can be measured by the degradation of the adversary C2. Defensively, effectiveness can be measured by retention of friendly forces C2 and survivability. The effectiveness of destructive assets can be measured by analyzing the effect on the enemy. The desired impact will be specified in the overall objectives provided by the JFC.

EW jammers vary in effective range, power, and modulation. EM radiations can be aimed and focused, but do not stop at definitive geographic boundaries or discrete altitudes. Theater EM spectrum (frequency) interface deconfliction procedures are necessary to minimize mutual interference and degradation of friendly efforts. Frequency management is enhanced if:

- Jammer system design includes directional antennas.

- Capabilities exist to lockout frequencies.

- Friendly forces state realistic restricted frequency requirements.

- A command and control process exists which is responsive to real-time frequency changes.

Intelligence Support

Accurate and timely intelligence is the foundation for effective EW planning and employment. Intelligence supports EW through several functions. First, constant analysis by various scientific and technical centers guards against hostile technical surprise. Second, indications and warning (I&W) centers provide tactical and strategic warning to friendly forces. Third, intelligence continually monitors threat systems to support reprogramming of all systems. Fourth, intelligence supports mission planning.

Specifically, intelligence supports EW by providing a technical threat description and a tailored threat environment description. Electronic warfare planning requires parametric and employment data, modeling and simulation tools, and mission planning tools to prioritize targets and defense tasks. All-source intelligence assets are required to support both offensive and defensive EW planning. To be of value, these assets must provide timely intelligence and be responsive to the commander's needs. Intelligence support includes establishing and maintaining comprehensive support databases as well as looking at scientific and technical intelligence and general military intelligence capabilities. Intelligence information must be filtered, integrated, and evaluated so the EW planners and decision makers are not overloaded with excessive or meaningless data.

Logistics Support

Readiness and sustainability of electronic assets are directly related to the quality of logistics planning. EW logistics programs should be developed in balance with modernization efforts and the operating capability each category of resources provides. Emphasis must be on total effectiveness to maximize EW capabilities.

EMPLOYMENT

General

The employment of EW capabilities to affect an adversary can yield a tremendous advantage to US military forces. EW objectives must be clearly established, support overall national and military objectives, and include identifiable indicators of success.

Combatant Commanders

Combatant commanders must carefully consider the potential of EW. Combatant commanders should:

✪ Integrate EW capabilities into deliberate and crisis action planning in accordance with appropriate policy and doctrine.

✪ Ensure maximum coordination among EW and other information operations intelligence and communications support activities to maximize effect and to reduce electronic fratricide.

✪ Incorporate EW tactics, techniques, and procedures into exercises and training events using the joint training process.

✪ Identify EW capability requirements and submit appropriate mission needs statements.

✪ Develop EW intelligence requirements in support of all pertinent OPLANs.

✪ Identify EW education and training requirements.

Integration with friends and allies is vital for successful use of EW. This HARM-equipped German Air Force PANAVIA TORNADO was part of NATO forces used in Operation ALLIED FORCE.

EW Applications Across the Spectrum of Combat

EW may be conducted in a variety of situations and circumstances across the range of military operations. **The decision to employ EW should be based not only on overall joint campaign or operation objectives, but also on the risks of possible adversary responses and other potential effects on the campaign or operation.** Based on an understanding of the tenets of EW discussed in chapter two, the employment of EW must include the consideration of several factors. Several EW applications may escalate use of the EM spectrum. For example, low orders of EW activity such as collection or exploitation have different consequences than lethal SEAD options. The Air Force may conduct operations across the different levels of war, and these operations may be affected by the EM spectrum. Included is a wide range of missions ranging from peacetime operations to war. The application of EW in military operations other than war (MOOTW) will probably be different. *It is a theater commander's responsibility to determine the level of EW application to operations under his control.*

Military Operations Other Than War

These missions may be operations into friendly nations; however, some nation-states are unstable and may include elements that are actively hostile toward the United States. In other situations, political or international considerations may require air operations to be conducted within known threat areas. Terrorist and criminal groups may possess man portable air defense systems (MANPADs) and other IR/electro-optical systems. The employment of flares and IR jammers may become an operational requirement to counter these threats during peaceful missions to these friendly nations. Several EW applications may be available for MOOTW. EW assets may be available for tasking for a variety of missions. Nearly all-nonlethal options are available, but it is the commander's responsibility to define these options in the ROE operation order (OPORD) or other governing directive. Although electronic attack options, such as communications and radar jamming are generally considered hostile, they may be necessary to protect the tasked forces.

Combat Operations

A properly constructed force package that includes EW enhances the probability of survival of all forces. It is unlikely that combat air and space operations will be able to completely avoid enemy defenses since they usually defend the desired targets. The density and potential lethality of the adversary air defense system may challenge mission effectiveness and the survivability of Air Force assets. At the tactical level, mission planning tries to strike the appropriate balance between mission accomplishment and force survival. Thorough planning at the operational level gives tactical commanders the proper tools to allow them to strike that balance.

BEKAA VALLEY (1982)

Russian built SA-9 like those used by Syria

On 9 June the IAF [Israeli Air Force] took on the Syrian air defenses in the Bekaa Valley with a complex yet carefully planned, coordinated, and executed attack. The Israelis used air- and ground-launched drones as decoys to activate Syrian radar. This allowed the Israeli EC-135s to obtain the location and frequency of the Syrian radars and in turn to rapidly relay this information to strike ele- ments. The Israelis thereby coupled real-time intelligence with rapid response to give their pilots precise locations of the SAMs and accurate tuning information for their jamming equipment. In the electronics war, the IAF used ECM pods, chaff rockets, possibly chaff from drones, and standoff jammers in CH-53, Boeing 707, and Arava transports. The Israeli airmen employed diversionary tactics, precise timing, sharply executed low-level tactics, and weapons such as ARMs, standoff weapons, iron bombs, and cluster munitions. In addition, the Israelis used a new surface-to-surface ARM, the WOLF missile. Ground forces fired artillery, launched ground assaults along the front, and just before the air attack took out a control center with a commando raid. The Syrians did not help their own cause, as they failed to dig in, poorly sited their radar, and ignited smoke screens that guided rather than confused the IAF. On the first day, the IAF destroyed 17 missile batteries and severely damaged two others. The Syrians pushed more SAM units into the Bekaa Valley, but to no avail. On the second day of the action, the IAF destroyed 11 more missile batteries. On 24 July the Israelis knocked out three batteries of SA-8s. A few days later, they destroyed some SA-9s. Reportedly, the IAF destroyed four SA-9 batteries in September.

Kenneth P. Werrell
Archie, Flak, AAA, and SAM

CHAPTER FIVE

EQUIP AND SUSTAIN

GENERAL

Air Force MAJCOMS are responsible to train and equip forces for employment by war-fighting joint force commanders (JFCs). In the process of equipping forces for EW, MAJCOMs must plan for, acquire, and field the parts, supplies, munitions, support equipment, support personnel, and communications infrastructure to sustain the EW capabilities of forces deployed or in garrison.

SYSTEM ENGINEERING

The ALQ-131 is an integrated system that has been updated to counter new and evolving threats.

System design should be driven by user requirements, current and projected threats, and concept of operations. To achieve this versatility, system design must be generic, robust, and easily expanded or modified to meet the threat. EW systems should be an integral part of the weapon system design. EW systems should be designed to accommodate any changes necessary to counter new and evolving threats. These design features ensure EW equipment is not only reactive but also anticipatory of threats designed to counter US responses. EW systems must be able to operate in a dense environment of both friendly and hostile systems. A means of maintaining security for possible war reserve modes must be incorporated in the system design to avoid compromise of our system capability. EW systems are subject to unintended interactions or mutual interference. This may come from other systems on the same platform, other aircraft, and other systems operating throughout the theater. Compatibility, interoperability, and frequency deconfliction of EW systems must be integrated across the electronic battlespace.

EFFECTIVE ELECTRONIC PROTECTION (EP)

EW systems evolve continuously as engineers develop improved capabilities and countermeasures to hostile capabilities. All weapons systems (not just EW systems) must have effective EP to operate in a hostile EW environment. Friendly forces expanded use and reliance on new technologies in the fields of communication and navigation have spotlighted the critical need to develop robust EP programs. Systems in development must include EP considerations at the beginning of the design cycle and be able to accept EP updates (hardware and software) to keep pace with the evolving EW threat. Continuous intelligence support is required to look for evolutionary and revolutionary developments in adversary threat systems so that the appropriate EP can be designed and deployed.

COMMUNICATIONS PLANS

Communications plans are directly related to electronic warfare plans. Communications plans provide for redundancy, workarounds, and regeneration of required friendly communications systems. Communications staff participation is required when EW frequency deconfliction and defensive information operations plans are worked. Communications support is critical for effective intelligence support and reprogramming actions for EW systems.

REPROGRAMMING AND ELECTRONIC DATABASE SUPPORT

EW operations demand large amounts of data on US and friendly systems and operations in addition to intelligence support on hostile forces. Programming and reprogramming EW systems and targeting work are based on parametric databases, EOB, and communications network databases. **An accurate and available intelligence base and the tools necessary to use the intelligence information are the foundation for effective EW planning and employment.** These databases are developed from US and friendly data exchanges and all-source intelligence collection and reporting. An EW system's flexibility depends on its capability to adapt to changing threats. EW systems depend on rapid reprogramming, which is enabled by rapid communication of intelligence data to operators and reprogramming centers, where updated mission software is created and transmitted to the field. This portion of the electronic warfare integrated reprogramming (EWIR) process depends on MAJCOM, system program office (SPO), Air Logistics Center (ALC), and reprogramming center support. The COMAFFOR should ensure the reprogramming process is accomplished for Air Force forces. In addition, if the COMAFFOR is also designated by the JFC as the JFACC, then that commander should ensure that reprogramming is done for all air and space forces assigned to the joint force.

INTELLIGENCE SUPPORT

An accurate and available intelligence base is the foundation for effective EW planning and employment. Intelligence supports EW by using various scientific and technical centers to guard against hostile technical surprise. I&W centers provide tactical and strategic warning for friendly forces. Also, intelligence monitors threat systems to support reprogramming and assist in mission planning.

CHAPTER SIX

EDUCATION AND TRAINING

> *In the profession of war the rules of the art are never violated without drawing punishment from the enemy who is delighted to find us at fault. An officer can spare himself many mistakes by improving himself.*
>
> **Frederick the Great**

Effective employment of EW depends on commanders, aircrews, and planners understanding EW system capabilities. To achieve this they must be well versed in the integration of EW at all levels of operations. Specialized education and realistic training in IO execution and EW employment achieve this objective. Specialized schools or classes are a valuable tool that can provide commanders, operations staffs, and operators with in-depth IO and EW skills. Education provides in-depth knowledge of theories of EW, which allow commanders and aircrews to creatively adapt to the dynamics of warfare. Training provides specific skills to be employed in time critical situations. Both are essential to success in war.

EDUCATION

Basic

High levels of proficiency are required for everyone involved with electronic warfare employment. All aircrews must receive basic EW education through unit-initiated programs. Aircrews should also attend major weapons system (MWS) specific training courses in order to gain the required in-depth knowledge of employing EW from their MWS. Examples include Fighter Electronic Combat Officers Course FECOC, (which is appropriate for A-10, F-16, F-15C/E and F-117 aircrews) and each of the airframe specific courses offered by Air Education and Training Command (AETC), both pipeline and upgrade training. Other specialties must be familiar with EW principles and employment in order to design and acquire useful systems, provide intelligence support, reprogram mission data, and perform other critical support and planning tasks. Additionally, practitioners of EW should try to attend the many joint/NATO EW courses that are available. Our sister Services and coalition partners have valuable experience that the USAF can learn from.

Advanced

Air operations staffs require specialized and comprehensive education training to acquire essential, unique skills. **These individuals are key elements for the effective integration of EW at all levels of the air campaign.** They must have an in-depth knowledge of national assets, and an understanding of targeting, so they can provide the commander with an EW package tailored to the operational objectives. Attendance of a JAOC initial qualification training course is recommended. Additionally, attendance of the USAF Electronic Warfare Coordinator course is highly recommended.

In this time of electronic media it would be remiss to forget the many excellent training and resource sites available on the worldwide web. Each of the major EW centers has such a website. These websites require SECRET Internet Protocol Router Network (SIPRNET) access, but they provide a wealth of technical and tactical information.

Senior

Senior officers must be well versed in the basic tenets of air and space EW employment and integration. Not only are they tasked as commanders for air operations during times of conflict, they are also involved with critical decisions on equipping, sustaining, and employing our forces to meet national objectives.

TRAINING

Training must have attainable objectives that are specific, relevant, and necessary for combat. Employment of EW during training should be accomplished in a realistic combat environment and should include operations with actual combat equipment. Employment restraints and limited resources are serious impediments to effective EW training. A review of deficiencies noted from past operations and exercises provides a valuable training resource. Emphasis should be placed on evaluating EW tactics, procedures, and safety constraints to optimize EW employment.

Electronic warfare training must be emphasized on a continuing basis (daily, weekly, quarterly, etc.) and must include all personnel who may encounter direct or indirect, friendly or hostile, EW situations. **EW impacts personnel in many areas to include: flight operations, air weapons, communications, intelligence, maintenance, security, and other operations and support functions.** Each training exercise must include EW objectives and EW assets. Strategic, and to a degree, operational level staff training can be achieved through gaming and simulation. Effective tactical training can only be achieved through live coordination and employment of actual EW assets.

Unit training should include enemy threat system characteristics, capabilities, and limitations. Unit training should also include, to the maximum extent possible, joint and coalition assets as well as organic USAF systems. **Operators must train against an IADS that includes all types of threats: surface-to-air, air-to-air, and electronic warfare systems.** Proficiency must be maintained in the operation of EW equipment as well as the employment of EW tactics both USAF and joint/coalition. Training should be realistic, based on accurate threat capabilities, and must provide accurate and rapid feedback to the trainees. The motto of EW training remains: **"Train with EW, Fight with EW."**

At the Heart of Warfare lies doctrine . . .

Suggested Readings

CJCSI 3210.01, *Joint Information Warfare Policy*

CJCSM 3212.01, *Performing Electronic Attack in the United States and Canada for Tests, Training, and Exercises*

DOD Directive S-3600.1, *Information Operations*

JP 3-13, *Joint Doctrine for Information Operations*

JP 3-13.1, *Joint Doctrine for Command and Control Warfare*

JP 3-51, *Joint Doctrine for Electronic Warfare*

JP 3-58, *Joint Doctrine for Military Deception*

Global Engagement: A Vision for the 21st Century Air Force

De Arcangelis, Mario. *Electronic Warfare: From the Battle of Tsushima to the Falklands and Lebanon Conflicts* (Poole, Dorset: Blandford Press). 1985.

Munro, Neil. *The Quick and the Dead: Electronic Combat and Modern Warfare* (New York: St Martin's Press). 1991.

Price, Alfred. *The History of US Electronic Warfare, Volume I* (The Association of Old Crowes). 1984.

Price, Alfred. *The History of US Electronic Warfare, Volume II* (The Association of Old Crowes). 1989.

Werrell, Kenneth P. *Archie, Flak, AAA, and SAM* (Maxwell AFB, AL: Air University Press) 1988.

Glossary

Abbreviations and Acronyms

AAA	antiaircraft artillery
ACO	airspace control order
ACQ	acquisition
ADCON	administrative control
AETC	Air Education and Training Command
AETF	air and space expeditionary task force
AFDD	Air Force Doctrine Document
AFFOR	Air Force forces
AFIWC	Air Force Information Warfare Center
ALC	Air Logistics Center
ANG	Air National Guard
AO	area of operations
ATO	air tasking order
C2	command and control
CAOC	Combined Air Operations Center
CFACC	Combined Force Air Component Commander
CJCSI	Chairman Joint Chiefs of Staff Instruction
COMAFFOR	Commander, Air Force Forces
COMINT	communications intelligence
COMSEC	communications security
CPD	Combat Plans Division
DCI	defensive counterinformation
DE	directed energy
DEW	directed-energy warfare
DOD	Department of Defense
DSO	defensive systems officer
EA	electronic attack
ECM	electronic countermeasures
ECO	electronic combat officer
EEI	essential elements of information
ELINT	electronics intelligence
EM	electromagnetic
EMCON	emission control
EOB	electronic order of battle
EP	electronic protection
ES	electronic warfare support
EW	electronic warfare
EW/GCI	early warning/ground-controlled intercept

EWIR	electronic warfare integrated reprogramming
EWO	**electronic warfare officer**
FDS	foundational doctrine statement
GCI	ground-controlled intercept
GPS	ground positioning system
HARM	high-speed antiradiation missile
HUMINT	human intelligence
IADS	integrated air defense system
I&W	indications and warning
IIW	information-in-warfare
IO	information operations
IR	infrared
ISR	intelligence, surveillance, and reconnaissance
JAOC	joint air operations center
JAOP	joint air operations plan
JFACC	joint force air and space component commander
JFC	joint force commander
JP	joint publication
JRFL	joint restricted frequency list
JSTARS	joint surveillance, target attack radar system
JTF	joint task force
MAJCOM	major command
MANPAD	man portable air defense system
MIJI	meaconing, interference, jamming and intrusion
MOOTW	military operations other than war
NAF	numbered air force
NATO	North Atlantic Treaty Organization
OCI	offensive counterinformation
OPCON	operational control
OPLAN	operation plan
OPORD	operation order
OPSEC	operations security
PRF	pulse repetition frequency
RFI	radio frequency interference
ROE	rules of engagement

RWR	radar warning receiver
SAM	surface-to-air missile
SEAD	suppression of enemy air defenses
SIGINT	signals intelligence
SOF	special operations forces
SPO	system program office
TACON	tactical control
UAV	unmanned aerial vehicle
USAFR	United States Air Force Reserve

Definitions

administrative control.   Direction or exercise of authority over subordinate or other organizations in respect to administration and support, including organization of Service forces, control of resources and equipment, personnel management, unit logistics, individual and unit training, readiness, mobilization, demobilization, discipline, and other matters not included in the operational missions of the subordinate or other organizations. Also called **ADCON.** (JP 1-02)

air tasking order.   A method used to task and disseminate to components, subordinate units, and command and control agencies projected sorties, capabilities, and/or forces to targets and specific missions.   Normally provides specific instructions to include call signs, targets, controlling agencies, etc., as well as general instructions. Also called **ATO.** (JP 1-02)

antiradiation missile.   A missile which homes passively on a radiation source.   Also called **ARM.** (JP 1-02)

chaff. Radar confusion reflectors consisting of thin, narrow metallic strips of various lengths and frequency responses, used to reflect echoes for confusion purposes. (JP 1-02) [NOTE: Most of today's chaff consists of aluminum-coated glass fiber.]

command and control.   The exercise of authority and direction by a properly designated commander over assigned and attached forces in the accomplishment of the mission. Command and control functions are performed through an arrangement of personnel, equipment, communications, facilities, and procedures employed by a commander in planning, directing, coordinating, and controlling forces and operations in the accomplishment of the mission. Also called **C2.** (JP 1-02)

command and control system.   The facilities, equipment, communications, procedures, and personnel essential to a commander for planning, directing, and controlling operations of assigned forces pursuant to the missions assigned. (JP 1-02)

communications deception. Use of devices, operations, and techniques with the intent of confusing or misleading the user of a communications link or a navigation system. (JP 1-02)

communications intelligence. Technical information and intelligence derived from foreign communications by other than the intended recipients. Also called **COMINT.** (JP 1-02)

communications security. The protection resulting from all measures designed to deny unauthorized persons information of value that might be derived from the possession and study of telecommunications, or to mislead unauthorized persons in their interpretation of the results of such possession and study. Also called **COMSEC.** Communications security includes: cryptosecurity, transmission security, emission security, and physical security of communications security materials and information.

a. **cryptosecurity**—The component of communications security that results from the provision of technically sound cryptosystems and their proper use.

b. **transmission security**—The component of communications security that results from all measures designed to protect transmissions from interception and exploitation by means other than cryptanalysis.

c. **emission security**—The component of communications security that results from all measures taken to deny unauthorized persons information of value that might be derived from intercept and analysis of compromising emanations from crypto-equipment and telecommunications systems.

d. **physical security**—The component of communications security that results from all physical measures necessary to safeguard classified equipment, material, and documents from access thereto or observation thereof by unauthorized persons. (JP 1-02)

concept of operations. A verbal or graphic statement, in broad outline, of a commander's assumptions or intent in regard to an operation or series of operations. The concept of operations frequently is embodied in campaign plans and operation plans; in the latter case, particularly when the plans cover a series of connected operations to be carried out simultaneously or in succession. The concept is designed to give an overall picture of the operation. It is included primarily for additional clarity of purpose. Also called **commander's concept** or **CONOPS.** (JP 1-02)

control. 1. Authority that may be less than full command exercised by a commander over part of the activities of subordinate or other organizations. 2. In mapping, charting, and photogrammetry, a collective term for a system of marks or objects on the Earth or on a map or a photograph, whose positions or elevations, or both, have been or will be determined. 3. Physical or psychological pressures exerted with the intent to assure that an agent or group will respond as directed. 4. An indicator governing the distribution and use of documents, information, or material. Such indicators are the subject of intelligence community agreement and are specifically defined in appropriate regulations. See also **administrative control, operational control, tactical control.** (JP 1-02)

counterinformation. Counterinformation seeks to establish a desired degree of control in information functions that permits friendly forces to operate at a given time or place without prohibitive interference by the opposing force. Also called **CI.** (AFDD 2-5)

countermeasures. That form of military science that, by the employment of devices and/or techniques, has as its objective the impairment of the operational effectiveness of enemy activity. See also **electronic warfare.** (JP 1-02)

deception. Those measures designed to mislead the enemy by manipulation, distortion, or falsification of evidence to induce the enemy to react in a manner prejudicial to the enemy's interests. (JP 1-02)

defensive counterinformation. Activities which are conducted to protect and defend friendly information and information systems. Also called **DCI.**

directed energy. An umbrella term covering technologies that relate to the production of a beam of concentrated electromagnetic energy or atomic or subatomic particles. Also called **DE.** (JP 1-02)

directed-energy warfare. Military action involving the use of directed-energy weapons, devices, and countermeasures to either cause direct damage or destruction of enemy equipment, facilities, and personnel, or to determine, exploit, reduce, or prevent hostile use of the electromagnetic spectrum through damage, destruction, and disruption. It also includes actions taken to protect friendly equipment, facilities, and personnel and retain friendly use of the electromagnetic spectrum. Also called **DEW.** (JP 1-02)

electromagnetic deception. The deliberate radiation, reradiation, alteration, suppression, absorption, denial, enhancement, or reflection of electromagnetic energy in a manner intended to convey misleading information to an enemy or to enemy electromagnetic-dependent weapons, thereby degrading or neutralizing the enemy's combat capability. Among the types of electromagnetic deception are:

    a. **manipulative electromagnetic deception**—Actions to eliminate revealing, or convey misleading, electromagnetic telltale indicators that may be used by hostile forces;

    b. **simulative electromagnetic deception**—Actions to simulate friendly, notional, or actual capabilities to mislead hostile forces;

    c. **imitative electromagnetic deception**—The introduction of electromagnetic energy into enemy systems that imitates enemy emissions. See also **electronic warfare.** (JP 1-02)

electromagnetic environmental effects. The impact of the electromagnetic environment upon the operational capability of military forces, equipment, systems, and platforms. It encompasses all electromagnetic disciplines, including electromagnetic compatibility and electromagnetic interference; electromagnetic vulnerability; electromagnetic pulse; electronic protection, hazards of electromagnetic radiation to personnel, ordnance, and volatile materials; and natural phenomena effects of lightning and precipitation-static. Also called **E3.** (JP 1-02)

electromagnetic interference. Any electromagnetic disturbance that interrupts, obstructs, or otherwise degrades or limits the effective performance of electronics and electrical equipment. It can be induced intentionally, as in some forms of electronic warfare, or unintentionally, as a result of spurious emissions and responses, intermodulation products, and the like. Also called **EMI.** (JP 1-02)

electromagnetic intrusion. The intentional insertion of electromagnetic energy into transmission paths in any manner, with the objective of deceiving operators or of causing confusion. See also **electronic warfare.** (JP 1-02)

electromagnetic jamming. The deliberate radiation, reradiation, or reflection of electromagnetic energy for the purpose of preventing or reducing an enemy's effective use of the electromagnetic spectrum, and with the intent of degrading or neutralizing the enemy's combat capability. (JP 1-02)

electromagnetic pulse. The electromagnetic radiation from a strong electronic pulse, most commonly caused by a nuclear explosion that may couple with electrical or electronic systems to produce damaging current and voltage surges. Also called **EMP.** See also **electromagnetic radiation.** (JP 1-02)

electromagnetic radiation. Radiation made up of oscillating electric and magnetic fields and propagated with the speed of light. Includes gamma radiation, X-rays, ultraviolet, visible, and infrared radiation, and radar and radio waves. (JP 1-02)

electromagnetic spectrum. The range of frequencies of electromagnetic radiation from zero to infinity. It is divided into 26 alphabetically designated bands. See also **electronic warfare.** (JP 1-02)

electromagnetic vulnerability. The characteristics of a system that cause it to suffer a definite degradation (incapability to perform the designated mission) as a result of having been subjected to a certain level of electromagnetic environmental effects. Also called **EMV.** (JP 1-02)

electronic attack. See **electronic warfare.** (JP 1-02)

electronic intelligence. Technical and geolocation intelligence derived from foreign non-communications electromagnetic radiations emanating from other than nuclear detonations or radioactive sources. Also called **ELINT.** (JP 1-02)

electronics security. The protection resulting from all measures designed to deny unauthorized persons information of value that might be derived from their interception and study of noncommunications electromagnetic radiations, e.g., radar. (JP 1-02)

electronic warfare. Any military action involving the use of electromagnetic and directed energy to control the electromagnetic spectrum or to attack the enemy. Also called **EW.** The three major subdivisions within electronic warfare are: electronic attack, electronic protection, and electronic warfare support.

a. **electronic attack.** That division of electronic warfare involving the use of electromagnetic energy, directed energy, or antiradiation weapons to attack personnel, facilities, or equipment with the intent of degrading, neutralizing, or destroying enemy combat capability. Also called **EA.** EA includes: 1) actions taken to prevent or reduce an enemy's effective use of the electromagnetic spectrum, such as jamming and electromagnetic deception, and 2) employment of weapons that use either electromagnetic or directed energy as their primary destructive mechanism (lasers, radio frequency weapons, particle beams).

b. **electronic protection.** That division of electronic warfare involving passive and active means taken to protect personnel, facilities, and equipment from any effects of friendly or enemy employment of electronic warfare that degrade, neutralize, or destroy friendly combat capability. Also called **EP.**

c. **electronic warfare support.** That division of electronic warfare involving actions tasked by, or under direct control of, an operational commander to search for, intercept, identify, and locate or localize sources of intentional and unintentional radiated electromagnetic energy for the purpose of immediate threat recognition, targeting, planning, and conduct of future operations. Thus, electronic warfare support provides information required for decisions involving electronic warfare operations and other tactical actions such as threat avoidance, targeting, and homing. Also called **ES.** Electronic warfare support data can be used to produce signals intelligence, provide targeting for electronic or destructive attack, and produce measurement and signature intelligence. (JP 1-02)

electronic warfare integrated reprogramming. A systematic decision-making tool for operational commanders. It gives all Air Force units a timely and accurate means to respond to expected and unexpected electronic emissions, changes in air defense tactics, and unique mission requirements. Theses EWIR responsibilities include procedures for changes in tactics, employment guidance, electronic warfare equipment (software/hardware), aircrew training and training devices (i.e. threat simulators, threat emitters) and other support systems. Also called **EWIR.**

electro-optics. The technology associated with those components, devices and systems which are designed to interact between the electromagnetic (optical) and the electric (electronic) state. (JP 1-02)

emission control. The selective and controlled use of electromagnetic, acoustic, or other emitters to optimize command and control capabilities while minimizing, for operations security: a. detection by enemy sensors; b. mutual interference among friendly systems; and/or c. enemy interference with the ability to execute a military deception plan. Also called **EMCON.** (JP 1-02)

essential elements of information. The critical items of information regarding the enemy and the environment needed by the commander by a particular time to relate with other available information and intelligence in order to assist in reaching a logical decision. Also called **EEI.** (JP 1-02)

information. 1. Facts, data, or instructions in any medium or form. 2. The meaning that a human assigns to data by means of the known conventions used in their representation. (JP 1-02)

information attack. Any activity taken to manipulate or destroy an adversary's information systems without necessarily changing visibly the physical entity within which it resides. (AFDD 1-2)

information-in-warfare. A set of information operations functions that provides commanders battlespace situational awareness across the spectrum of conflict and range of air and space operations. Information-in-warfare functions involve the Air Force's extensive capabilities to provide awareness throughout the range of military operations based on integrated intelligence, surveillance, and reconnaissance (ISR) assets; its information collection/dissemination activities; and its global navigation and positioning, weather, and communications capabilities. Also called **IIW.** (AFDD 2-5)

information operations. Use of offensive and defensive information means to degrade, destroy, and exploit an adversary's information-based process while protecting one's own. Also called **IO.** (JP 1-02). The Air Force believes that in practice a more useful working definition is: *[Those actions taken to gain, exploit, defend or attack information and information systems and include both information-in-warfare and information warfare.]* {Italicized definition in brackets applies only to the Air Force and is offered for clarity}.

information superiority. That degree of dominance in the information domain which permits the conduct of operations without effective opposition. Also called **IS.** (JP 1-02) The Air Force prefers to cast 'superiority' as a state of relative advantage, not a capability, and views IS as: *[That degree of dominance in the information domain which allows friendly forces the ability to collect, control, exploit, and defend information without effective opposition.]* {Italicized definition in brackets applies only to the Air Force and is offered for clarity.}

information system. The entire infrastructure, organization, personnel, and components that collect, process, store, transmit, display, disseminate, and act on information. See also **information, information warfare.** (JP 1-02)

information warfare. Information operations conducted during time of crisis or conflict to achieve or promote specific objectives over a specific adversary or adversaries. Also called **IW.** (JP 1-02) *[Information operations conducted to defend one's own information and information systems, or to attack and affect an adversary's information and information systems.]* {Italicized definition in brackets applies only to the Air Force and is offered for clarity.}

intelligence, surveillance, and reconnaissance. Integrated capabilities to collect, process, exploit and disseminate accurate and timely information that provides the battlespace awareness necessary to successfully plan and conduct operations. Also called **ISR.** (This is an Air Force term as applied to the scope for this AFDD).

interference. See **electromagnetic interference** (JP 1-02) *[Interference is any electrical disturbance that causes undesirable responses in electronic equipment.]* {Italicized definition in brackets applies only to the Air Force and is offered for clarity.}

intrusion. Movement of a unit or force within another nation's specified operational area outside of territorial seas and territorial airspace for surveillance or intelligence gathering in time of peace or tension. See **electromagnetic intrusion.** (JP 1-02) *[Intrusion is intentionally inserting electromagnetic energy into transmission paths in any manner. The object is to deceive equipment operators or cause confusion. The enemy conducts intrusion operations against us by inserting false information into our receiver paths. This false information may consist of voice instructions, ghost targets, coordinates for fire missions, or even rebroadcasting or prerecorded data transmissions.]* {Italicized definition in brackets applies only to the Air Force and is offered for clarity.}

jamming. See **electromagnetic jamming.** (JP 1-02) *[Jamming is deliberately radiating, reradiating, or reflecting electromagnetic energy to impair the use of electronic devices, equipment, or systems. The enemy conducts jamming operations against us to prevent us from effectively employing our radios, radars, NAVAIDs, satellites, and eletro-optics.]* {Italicized definition in brackets applies only to the Air Force and is offered for clarity.}

joint air operations plan. A plan for a connected series of joint air operations to achieve the joint force commander's objectives within a given time and theater of operations. (JP 1-02).

joint force. A general term applied to a force composed of significant elements, assigned or attached, of two or more Military Departments, operating under a single joint force commander. (JP 1-02)

joint force air component commander *[joint force air and space component commander].* The commander within a unified command, subordinate unified command, or joint task force responsible to the establishing commander for making recommendations on the proper employment of assigned, attached, and/or made available for tasking air forces; planning and coordinating air operations; or accomplishing such operational missions as may be assigned. The joint force air component commander is given the authority necessary to accomplish missions and tasks assigned by the establishing commander. Also called **JFACC.** See also **joint force commander.** (JP 1-02) *[AFDDs 2-2 and 2-5 introduced the acronym JFASCC which is strictly an Air Force term to signify the Air Force commitment to developing a commander with both air and space knowledge. Subsequently (Jul 02), CSAF chose to revert back to JFACC (joint usage). For Air Force usage JFACC means Joint Force Air and Space Component Commander. See also AFDC Doctrine Watch #18]* {Italicized definition in brackets applies only to the Air Force and is offered for clarity.}

joint force commander. A general term applied to a combatant commander, subunified commander, or joint task force commander authorized to exercise combatant command (command authority) or operational control over a joint force. Also called **JFC.** (JP 1-02)

joint suppression of enemy air defenses. A broad term that includes all suppression of enemy air defense activities provided by one component of the joint force in support of another. Also called **J-SEAD.** (JP 1-02)

joint task force. A joint force that is constituted and so designated by the Secretary of Defense, a combatant commander, a subunified commander, or an existing joint task force commander. Also called **JTF.** (JP 1-02)

meaconing. A system of receiving radio beacon signals and rebroadcasting them on the same frequency to confuse navigation. The meaconing stations cause inaccurate bearings to be obtained by aircraft or ground stations. (JP 1-02) *[Successful enemy meaconing causes: 1. Aircraft to be lured into hot landing zones or enemy airspace 2. Bombers to expend ordnance on false targets. 3. Ground stations to receive inaccurate bearings or position locations.]* {Italicized definition in brackets applies only to the Air Force and is offered for clarity.}

military deception. Actions executed to deliberately mislead adversary military decision makers as to friendly military capabilities, intentions, and operations, thereby causing the adversary to take specific actions (or inactions) that will contribute to the accomplishment of the friendly mission. The five categories of military deception are as follows:

   a. **strategic military deception**—Military deception planned and executed by and in support of senior military commanders to result in adversary military policies and actions that support the originator's strategic military objectives, policies, and operations.

   b. **operational military deception**—Military deception planned and executed by and in support of operational-level commanders to result in adversary actions that are favorable to the originator's objectives and operations. Operational military deception is planned and conducted in a theater to support campaigns and major operations.

   c. **tactical military deception**—Military deception planned and executed by and in support of tactical commanders to result in adversary actions that are favorable to the originator's objectives and operations. Tactical military deception is planned and conducted to support battles and engagements.

   d. **Service military deception**—Military deception planned and executed by the Services that pertain to Service support to joint operations. Service military deception is designed to protect and enhance the combat capabilities of Service forces and systems.

   e. **military deception in support of operations security (OPSEC)**—Military deception planned and executed by and in support of all levels of command to support the prevention of the inadvertent compromise of sensitive or classified activities, capabilities, or intentions. Deceptive OPSEC measures are designed to distract foreign intelligence away from, or provide cover for, military operations and activities. See also **deception.** (JP 1-02)

offensive counterinformation. Offensive IO/IW activities which are conducted to control the information environment by denying, degrading, disrupting, destroying, and deceiving the adversary's information and information systems. Also called **OCI.** (AFDD 2-5)

operational control. Command authority that may be exercised by commanders at any echelon at or below the level of combatant command. Operational control is inherent in combatant command (command authority) and may be delegated within the command. When forces are transferred between combatant commands, the command relationship the gaining commander will exercise (and the losing commander will relinquish) over these forces must be specified by the Secretary of Defense. Operational control is the authority to perform those functions of command over subordinate forces involving organizing and employing commands and forces, assigning tasks, designating objectives, and giving authoritative direction necessary to accomplish the mission. Operational control includes authoritative direction over all aspects of military operations and joint training necessary to accomplish missions assigned to the command. Operational control should be exercised through the commanders of subordinate organizations. Normally this authority is exercised through subordinate joint force commanders and Service and/or functional component commanders. Operational control normally provides full authority to organize commands and forces and to employ those forces as the commander in operational control considers necessary to accomplish assigned missions; it does not, in and of itself, include authoritative direction for logistics or matters of administration, discipline, internal organization, or unit training. Also called OPCON. (JP 1-02)

operations security. A process of identifying critical information and subsequently analyzing friendly actions attendant to military operations and other activities to: a. identify those actions that can be observed by adversary intelligence systems; b. determine indicators that hostile intelligence systems might obtain that could be interpreted or pieced together to derive critical information in time to be useful to adversaries; and c. select and execute measures that eliminate or reduce to an acceptable level the vulnerabilities of friendly actions to adversary exploitation. Also called OPSEC. (JP 1-02)

radar. A radio detection device that provides information on range, azimuth and/or elevation of objects. (JP 1-02)

radar countermeasures. See electronic warfare; chaff. (JP 1-02)

radar coverage. The limits within which objects can be detected by one or more radar stations. (JP 1-02)

radar deception. See electromagnetic deception. (JP 1-02)

signals intelligence. 1. A category of intelligence comprising either individually or in combination all communications intelligence, electronic intelligence, and foreign instrumentation signals intelligence, however transmitted. 2. Intelligence derived from communications, electronic, and foreign instrumentation signals. Also called SIGINT. (JP 1-02)

suppression. Temporary or transient degradation by an opposing force of the performance of a weapons system below the level needed to fulfill its mission objectives. (JP 1-02)

suppression of enemy air defenses. That activity which neutralizes, destroys, or temporarily degrades surface-based enemy air defenses by destructive and/or disruptive means. Also called SEAD. (JP 1-02)

tactical control. Command authority over assigned or attached forces or commands, or military capability or forces made available for tasking, that is limited to the detailed direction and control of movements or maneuvers within the operational area necessary to accomplish missions or tasks assigned. Tactical control is inherent in operational control. Tactical control may be delegated to, and exercised at any level at or below the level of combatant command. When forces are transferred between combatant commands, the command relationship the gaining commander will exercise (and the losing commander will relinquish) over these forces must be specified by the Secretary of Defense. Tactical control provides sufficient authority for controlling and directing the application of force or tactical use of combat support assets within the assigned mission or task. Also called **TACON.** (JP 1-02)

window. Window is a historic British term for chaff that is occasionally referenced in various documents. See **chaff.**